THE RAILWAY ADVENTURES

PLACES, TRAINS, PEOPLE AND STATIONS

THE RAILWAY ADVENTURES

PLACES, TRAINS, PEOPLE AND STATIONS

VICKI PIPE & GEOFF MARSHALL

3 5 7 9 10 8 6 4 2

First published in 2018 by September Publishing

Maps and quaint scale by Liam Roberts
Design by Clarkevanmeurs Design and Martin Brown

Printed in Poland on paper from responsibly managed, sustainable sources by Hussar Books

ISBN 978-1-910463-87-1

September Publishing
www.septemberpublishing.org

CONTENTS

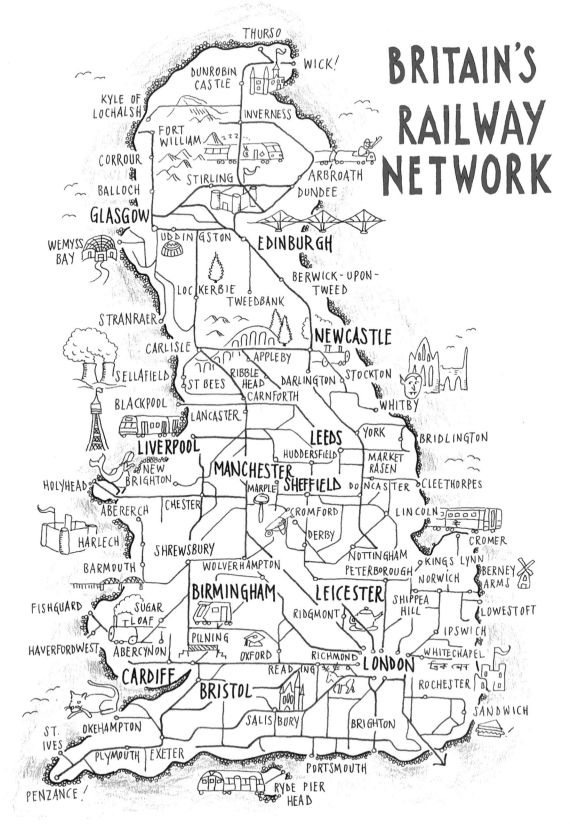

BRITAIN'S RAILWAY NETWORK

INTRODUCTION
OUR ALL THE STATIONS JOURNEY

During the spring and summer of 2017 we, that's Vicki and Geoff, undertook an adventure to travel to all 2,563 national railway stations in Great Britain. Crowdfunded by 1,564 people on Kickstarter, we captured photographs and posted them on social media and filmed the entire experience, sharing it with our followers on YouTube. Now we've written this book as we want to inspire you to get out there and have your own railway adventures too.

Vicki: For me it's the people that make the railways such an exciting place to explore. Railways have such a dramatic impact on our lives, they connect us to places and people that we would otherwise not think to reach out to. The process of travel and adventure helps us understand ourselves, our communities and the communities of others in a way no other activity can.

Geoff: I've always been fascinated by the infrastructure and the systems that make the railways work. Understanding timetables and how one facet of the system interconnects with another is a puzzle that never ceases to change, and I am constantly eager to learn how it all comes together.

Together we wanted to really see where the railways could take us, to bring to life the places and stations which for so long had just been indistinguishable names on a map. How pleasant is Pleasington? How awe-inspiring is Loch Awe? Is there really a Hall i' th' Wood? And who exactly are the 12 people using Shippea Hill station every year?

Another crucial factor was the realisation that Britain's railways are changing. In the next five to ten years, services that exist now will become twice if not three times as fast; some may not even exist at all. The trains we travel on will have been replaced and the idea that you can live in London and commute to Edinburgh may just have become a reality. Technology is advancing the way we shape our lives and how we travel at high speed (pun intended). We wanted to take our journey and document it for posterity, for people to look back on and understand what Britain's railways were like in 2017.

But we got more into the bargain. We met people who shared their time, their knowledge and their railway experiences more generously than we could have imagined. They gave us lifts, gifts and told us about their communities, how the railways affect them, the good and the bad. Where services are efficient opportunities flourish, in areas with more limited choices people can find themselves isolated. As the nucleus of many communities, the railways are not just a mode of transport, they have shaped the country and they continue to shape people's lives.

And the journey itself is sometimes the best part of all. Unlike travelling by car you don't have to choose a designated driver; that decision has already been taken care of. Everyone can be part of the adventure. Relax and spend time watching the landscape change through the window, share stories or plan the details of your day. It's in these moments that you might decide to be spontaneous and completely change your route – we made some of our best discoveries by getting out at unexpected places, just because we could. And, you never know who might be sitting just across the aisle from you. Chances are there will be someone local to where you're going, an expert who can tell you all the best places to visit, as well as which ones to avoid.

Be curious, ask questions and take your time – you never know what you might discover. Whether you go just a few stops further than normal on your daily commute, travel to the other side of the country or 'break your journey' to explore that interesting building/castle/statue/topiary you've always noticed from the train, *all* are an adventure.

To the trains!

CHAPTER 1

FIRST, CHOOSE YOUR <u>PLACE</u>

FIRST, CHOOSE YOUR <u>PLACE</u>

Of course, having a railway adventure isn't just about travelling on trains. It's about exploring the places the railways take you.

First, you have to choose where to alight, and with so many interesting areas to explore that is one of the most exciting and challenging aspects of the journey. While you can find loads of information online, we recommend using local knowledge. For our challenge, we asked for tips and suggestions from the Great British public on social media and, as it turns out, the public are incredibly passionate about where they live or used to live – the places they grew up, where they went to school or where they've visited their grandparents every Sunday for the last 20 years. Ask your friends and family, question your colleagues, you could even pop a message out into the Twittersphere. You will notice that while passions are predominantly positive, people also feel compelled to tell you where you shouldn't go – however, we found that unravelling *why* we shouldn't go somewhere often gave us more insight into that place's identity than those locations we were told were 'must see' (see Welsh Valleys, page 18).

We received literally hundreds of suggestions, and every single tip went into our 'Master Spreadsheet', but we knew there was no way we would be able to visit every place we'd been given. We quickly developed two key questions to help us decide where to alight:

1. Is it within walking distance (or a reasonable taxi ride) from the station?
2. How long have we got before the next train departs?

You don't even have to spend an entire day somewhere. If you ever find yourself with a 40-minute change over somewhere, you can most certainly fit in a 'mini' explore. It's easy to do this at the very central city stations, such as Birmingham, Glasgow and Cardiff, but it's also doable in smaller areas too, like Canterbury, Hinkley, Largs, Penmaen-mawr, and that's just for starters.

We often found that the activities we hadn't planned turned out to be the most interesting and exciting moments of the trip. If someone you are chatting to becomes very animated, or if you receive multiple 'YOU HAVE TO GO AND SEE . . .' tip-offs, always reroute if you can. Just like when we travelled through Derbyshire. Originally, we had planned to end our first day at Matlock; however, we'd received so many messages telling us that Cromford station (on the same branch) was used as the location for the cover of the 1995 Oasis single 'Some Might Say' that we simply couldn't ignore the opportunity to take a closer look.

Right | Our recreation of the Oasis single cover 'Some Might Say'. If only we'd have been able to find some fish.

Of course, your adventure doesn't have to be about historical sites or pop culture references. On our challenge we also wanted to explore the current status of the railways. To discover how they work, and work differently in different parts of the country, and also how they are used and what they are used for. The idea that the network provides something more to society than just a service from A to B is often overshadowed in day-to-day announcements about can-celled trains, changing franchises, performance statistics, timetable alterations or the costs involved in upgrading a line. But as Sir Peter Hendy, chair of Network Rail, told us when we asked him what he thinks the railways are for, 'It's very important people realise its huge place in the society and economy of the Britain we live and work in.' From the building of infrastructure and the systems that make the network run, to the people who work and use the railway as well as the connections between different places along the way, our adventure taught us there is almost no aspect of modern Britain that the railways do not impact.

Right | We met Sir Peter Hendy outside Euston station just a few weeks into our journey. Sir Peter was also a Kickstarter backer for the project, and adopted Dalston Junction and St Erth stations as his reward.

Discovering new locations, talking to local people, hearing stories that have shaped those places at different times and being able to see first-hand where it all happened, where it still happens, has given us a unique and comprehensive perspective of Britain which we never could have envisaged at the beginning of our adventure.

Every place, no matter how small or seemingly unpronounceable (Llanfairpwllgwyngyllgogerychwyrndrobwllllantysiliogogogoch), has a story to tell. Inevitably, that story is interwoven in some way with the arrival or departure of the railways (and often with castles too – seriously, there are loads of them).

In the nineteenth century, the arrival of the railway to the small fishing town of Looe in Cornwall created a more efficient alternative to canals for transporting copper ore from Bodmin Moor to South Wales (via ships docked in Looe harbour). But when the mining industry declined the railway continued running, transporting passengers instead of goods. It was a vital link for an otherwise isolated town and transformed the area and the prospects of those living there, as Looe became a much-desired tourist destination. In 2017 alone over 120,000 people made the journey to Looe – it is currently the 1,619th busiest station on the network!

Developments taking place on the network today effect a change much bigger than it might at first seem. Pilning station in Gloucestershire, once a hubbub of services and fully staffed (including up to 14 signallers operating the area's three signal boxes), provided routes in and out of Bristol and towards Cardiff. In 2006 services were cut to Saturdays only (one train in each direction) and then in 2016, even more devastating, this decreased to just two trains in one direction. The impact for the local community was significant, not only for local businesses or those getting to work, but particularly for young people who feel trapped in the surrounding small villages, unable to travel independently for school, college or to meet friends. However, locals have rallied to form an active campaign group, and Pilning Station Group fiercely fight for better and more frequent services.

Above | Picturesque Looe. The ferry to cross the East Looe River costs just 50p. That's right, 50 pence.

A change to the network is a change to the landscape, the economy and the opportunities available for people who live close by. In many cases, such as at Pilning, a change is almost as significant as when the railways first came into being. That the railways have a role to play in continuing to define our sense of identity and the places in which we live is incontrovertible.

Wherever you alight, and whatever adventures you look for when you arrive, destination is key when deciding your journey. In this chapter, we share with you some of the places and stories that resonated the most – which made us see things differently or that took us by surprise.

'I don't understand how we can still be in England'

Above | Porthminster Beach, just below St Ives station. Next stop, Greece!

St Ives

We visited St Ives on the very first day of our adventure. Knowing full well that we'd rarely have the luxury to stay as long anywhere else over the next three months, we eased ourselves in with a lengthy four hours (we know!) to take it all in.

Originally a prominent fishing port, it was the arrival of the railways in the nineteenth century, on a branch line from St Erth, which began St Ives' transformation into a popular tourist destination. And boy are we grateful that it did. As soon as we stepped off the train and turned to look out over the beach just below the station, Vicki's mouth dropped open: 'I don't understand how we can still be in England!' For the sea at St Ives is a stunning Mediterranean blue, something we had literally never seen in Britain before. *Vicki: Especially me! I went to school in Hunstanton, where at best the water is a light grey colour.*

And it's not just the sea which has an exotic feel. A haven for artists (YOU HAVE TO GO AND SEE Tate St Ives or the Barbara Hepworth Museum and Sculpture Garden), their influence can be felt throughout

ICE CREAM AND
CHIP THIEVES
OPERATE IN THIS AREA
SHIELD YOUR FOOD

BEWARE THE GULLS

DON'T FEED THEM · DON'T TEACH THEM St.Ives

Above | Our first but not our last encounter with the mighty gull.

the town in the many galleries and potteries jumbled together along the winding, hilly streets. These sit alongside unending independent shops, vegan cafés, ice cream cafés, regular cafés, restaurants and corner stores, some boasting trade for over a hundred years. All open, all welcoming and obliterating the phrase 'typical British seaside town'. Indeed, there is very little that is 'typical' about St Ives.

More than being an artistic centre, there is a sense of tranquillity about St Ives that seeps into you the moment you step off the train, and before you know it you're sat on a bench by the harbour, eating chips (or rather shielding them from the gulls) and content to watch the ships roll by. St Ives was the perfect place to start our journey, giving us a unique perspective from which to view the rest of the country. It shatters your expectations and epitomises the extreme contrasts that make up 'Great Britain'. Go from the Mediterranean haven of Cornwall to the hard-industrial landscapes of Yorkshire, then over to the meandering hills of Wales and up to the coarse, ragged crags of the Scottish Highlands. See urbanisation, remoteness, over-crowding and sparse wilderness, all of which are accessible by one common denominator: the railway.

Welsh Valleys

Everyone said to us that there's not much to see in the Welsh Valleys. Someone from the Valleys even told us, 'You know what you absolutely should do when you get to Merthyr Tydfil?' *'Ohh* tell us!' 'Leave.' 'Ah.'

However, far from making us dismiss the Valleys, we wanted to know more. What's wrong with the Welsh Valleys?

It's true, the towns and villages along the Valley Lines don't offer the same kind of obvious attractions that you get somewhere like Cardiff. What they do have, nevertheless, is a rich story to tell.

The Welsh Valleys were famous for ore and coal mining throughout the nineteenth and twentieth centuries. The livelihood of almost every family in the area was reliant on the work, support and community that

'Expect stories of strength and community'

Right | Artwork in Bank Square, Ebbw Vale. A reminder of the town's connection to the steel and coal industries.

these industries supplied. The railways were built to serve the mining villages, as well as the pits themselves. (We were sent a map of the Valleys pre-Beeching showing many more lines than even we had realised. Today only six lines remain.)

After a long period of struggle, battling against government closures, the decline of coal use and imports of ore from other countries, almost all the pits in Wales closed in the 1980s. Since then there have been high levels of unemployment in and around the towns and villages along the Valley Lines. Some families born into the mining industries have never worked again. Current lack of job opportunities, and the sparse nature of cultural engagement, entertainment and connection to other parts of Wales have given the Valleys a less than positive reputation. One of the train guards we chatted to told us that, faced with such challenging circumstances, young people often make their own entertainment on the railways, including train surfing – which we were staggered to realise is actually a real thing (Google it, but don't ever do it!), causing disruption and serious safety concerns.

While providing an, albeit illegal, distraction from the challenges of Valley life, the railways could offer up a tantalising opportunity for growth. They currently only provide direct services in and out of Cardiff, but with more services and better connections to places such as Swansea and Newport, the prospects for people living in the Valleys could change. With vision, the railways – first built to bring people to an already booming industry – could become the means by which new industries and opportunities grow.

Above | Treherbert station. Not always the end of the line.

Treherbert station, now the end of the line, was once the midpoint connecting the Taff Vale Railway and the Rhondda and Swansea Bay Railway, with a tunnel under the mountains linking one valley with the next. If this line was still operational, think about the opportunities for local people.

Once we had discovered both the history and the current challenges and campaigns, we gained a real sense of the richness of the Welsh Valleys. Yes, don't expect glitz and glamour or even shops and cafés open past 5 p.m. (except Greggs, top tip if you're in need of an emergency cup of tea in Ebbw Vale), but the hardships and changing fortunes along the Valley Lines are just as important to understand as more obvious places of interest.

If you visit the Welsh Valleys expect stories of strength and community and hope for the future. Also expect exceptionally friendly people, like Cerian from Aberdare (who gets another mention in chapter 4 because she's such a legend) who drove us to Treherbert over the incredibly beautiful Craig y Llyn, proving to us that the Valleys aren't just about industry!

Other points of interest along the line worth an explore include Ebbw Vale, which (as well as providing emergency tea) has a funicular elevator taking you from the station up to the town centre.

Whitby

Whitby is one of the country's secret gems. A place which, unless you live close by or have access to a car, you probably wouldn't make the effort to get to. It is rather stuck out on the north-east coast, an hour and a half from Middlesbrough by train. But by goodness, it is worth the journey.

In essence it's a lovely seaside town, where you can get a cracking portion of fish and chips (we recommend Magpies – other establishments are available) and a (£1)99p cone. Simultaneously it is also not your typical seaside town. It reminds us more of St Ives than Skegness, more North Berwick than Blackpool, but even those comparisons don't fully capture its distinctiveness.

There is a rich history to Whitby that permeates throughout: Viking raids, strong maritime traditions – epitomised by the presence of Captain Cook's lodgings; there was once even a controversial whaling industry which flourished during the eighteenth and nineteenth centuries. More than anything, however, Whitby echoes with a history that never actually existed – that of Bram Stoker's *Dracula*.

While visiting Whitby in the late 1800s, Bram Stoker was inspired by the ruins of the incredible Gothic-styled abbey, which continues to peer ominously over the town from its vantage point on East Cliff. Part of the novel is set in Whitby itself, where the character of Dracula

Right | Whitby's literary connection to Bram Stoker's *Dracula* is evident throughout the town.

arrives having travelled from Transylvania to spread the torment of the undead. It is even said that Stoker found the name of Dracula in a book at Whitby library.

It is a connection that is hard to shake as you walk around the town itself, encountering the quaint (a solid 8 out of 10 on the quaint scale) winding streets along the harbour. You can't help but picture the sea mist rolling out and bats screeching in the pre-dawn light. Even the steaming locomotive of the local North Yorkshire Moors Railway (which incidentally runs trains from Whitby to Grosmont where you can pick up the full heritage railway experience) adds to the sensation of a mysterious and literary past era.

This blurring of fact and fiction at Whitby is a different kind of tourism to the norm, subtler and in some ways more powerful, as it plays on your imagination. During our visit the abbey was busy with a constant stream of visitors and we wondered how many people were there simply because of the *Dracula* connection. We experienced something similar in only a few other places on our travels – Stratford-upon-Avon, for example, which uses the mysteries of Shakespeare's life to conjure up a history which may or may not have existed.

We don't think Whitby minds the connotations too much, having seen several reminders of the *Dracula* connection throughout the town, including posters for the biannual Whitby Goth Weekend and the more regularly conducted Dracula Experience tours and Paranormal Nights. It certainly isn't a detriment to the experience of the town; in fact it gives the town a real charm that left us unnaturally hungry for more . . .

Below | The haunting ruins of Whitby Abbey, now looked after by English Heritage.

'Echoes with a history that never actually existed'

Chapel-le-Dale

In the western hub of the Yorkshire Dales is the hamlet of Chapel-le-Dale. In the graveyard of St Leonard's church is a commemorative stone and plaque dedicated 'To the Memory of the many men, women and children resident in this Parish between 1870 and 1877 who died through accident or disease during the construction of the Settle–Carlisle Railway and who were buried in this churchyard.' Considered expendable by the company who employed them, they were buried in unmarked graves, their names forgotten to history. Their legacy, however, is still considered one of the greatest feats and features of Britain's railway, and includes the Ribblehead Viaduct.

While the viaduct itself is almost beyond description in its magnitude and sheer audacity, to stand under one of its 24 enduring arches in the driving Yorkshire rain gives you just a small sense of what it must have been like for those undertaking its life-threatening construction.

Chapel-le-Dale is a minuscule hamlet, a dozen or so houses and farm buildings along a single country lane. There is literally nothing

Below | The Ribblehead Viaduct – one of the most impressive and imposing features of railway infrastructure in Britain.

'Put our pleasure of travelling along the railways in sharp relief'

between you and the elements. Railway workers and their families would likely have been housed in and around both the hamlet and the building site of the viaduct in makeshift structures. While the perceptible danger was from construction of the line itself, deadlier for workers' wives and children were the illness and disease which spread quickly in such impoverished conditions.

It can be hard to imagine the hardships endured by those from the past when their circumstances and experiences are so disparate from our own. But standing in the isolated St Leonard's churchyard and observing the understated memorial to those who lost so much put our pleasure of travelling along the railway in sharp relief. While our adventure was about the current experience of Britain's railways, we discovered that there are some places where the past is simply inextricable from the present.

We encourage you to take a train to Ribblehead, but before you take a close-up look at the viaduct, why not make the short journey to Chapel-le-Dale (grab a taxi, or walk the two miles if the weather is nice), and spend a few moments to reflect on those unnamed who made so many of our journeys possible.

Merseyside

We wish we could have spent more time in Merseyside. A week, even two, probably wouldn't have been enough. Besides the incredible history and culture of the whole area, it is the people of Merseyside who made it one of the friendliest and most delightful places we visited.

On almost every train we took someone chatted to us. From guards and shoppers to busy commuters, cycling hobbyists and oil refinery workers, everyone was keen to share a story and point us in the direction of somewhere interesting to go.

When you think of Merseyside it's easy to automatically focus on the city of Liverpool itself; the Beatles, the docks and the liver birds – tick. In reality, Merseyside reaches from the Wirral (the peninsula south of the River Mersey), through Liverpool, Sefton (north-west of the city), Knowsley, (north-east of the city) and St Helens (north-east of Knowsley), all connected by the railways and all with rich and interwoven stories to tell. There is a friendly (or so it seemed to us) rivalry between all the districts, but most particularly between the Wirral and the city of Liverpool. It's a historical contention, but is still reflected in lots of subtle ways, from a choice of football allegiance to the nicknames we heard people reference in casual conversation or while on the phone. (We still haven't quite worked out the difference between Scousers, Plastic Scousers and Woollybacks – if you know please tweet us a Venn diagram so we can finally put that one to rest.)

As well as being incredibly inviting, Merseyside is a place of fascinating contrasts. The model village of Port Sunlight (which ricochets off the quaint scale), for example, was built by William Hesketh, one half of the Lever Brothers company (nineteenth and twentieth-century manufacturers of soap and other household products). Hesketh was an innovator in providing welfare, safe accommodation and high standards of living for his workers. The village is made up of over 900 incredible Grade II listed buildings and is protected by the Port Sunlight Trust. As we walked around its immaculately kept gardens, lawns and public spaces we felt enchanted. What a transformation this must have been for those employees, many of whom would have been used to more stereotypical Victorian factory conditions.

A few stops further up the line and a short walk from James Street station, however, is the International Slavery Museum, telling a very

'A place of continuous and fascinating contrasts'

Right | Sunlight Soap, the leading product of the Lever Brothers factory in Port Sunlight.

different humanitarian story. In the eighteenth century, the transatlantic slave trade saw a significant majority of all European slave ships leave from Liverpool, and the sobering fact is that until the abolition of the slave trade in 1807 a lot of Liverpool's wealth was made from the operation of slave ships. The museum explores this heart-wrenching story and discusses the real impact of slavery not just in Liverpool but around the world, past and present.

In contrast to the harsh realities of the past, Merseyside is also home to its share of nautical myths. These filter into your consciousness in places such as New Brighton, home to the Mermaid Trail, inspired by the local legend of the Black Rock Mermaid, who is said to have saved the life of local sailor John Robinson during a storm in exchange for his promise to visit her. But John failed to appear and so the mermaid

Above | Mermaid at New Brighton station.

called on her powers of the sea to bring John to her at Black Rock instead, where it is said you can still hear the voice of the mermaid singing and the sound of John Robinson calling to her.

In fact, such a vast proportion of Merseyside's towns are on or near the coast you'd be hard pushed not to find a stunning view across the sea or riverside. The local relationship to the sea is captured by Antony Gormley's installation *Another Place*, made up of 100 iron figures that stretch along the coast and out to sea (between Waterloo and Blundellsands & Crosby stations), at times appearing to dominate the sea and at other times overpowered by it.

Perhaps it is Merseyside's disparity of experiences within the region which has forged such strong a sense of community and a friendly atmosphere. It was certainly one of the most open and welcoming places we went to.

Glasgow

Until now, all our joint trips to Scotland had been to Edinburgh, mainly due to consecutive yearly visits to the Edinburgh Festival. When we thought of Scotland we thought of Edinburgh and its incomprehensibly busy streets (we really should make a visit when the festival isn't on). But Scotland is not just Edinburgh. There are the Highlands and the coast, and even the bits that don't have (and have never had – gasp!) railways. And then there is Glasgow.

We spent just over a week in Glasgow, the longest we stayed in any one place during our journey. We had estimated it would take five to six days to do all the suburban railways in the area, and we added on a couple of days for good measure in the hope that we could take a couple of days off and relax. (It was a minor revelation the first day we checked into our hotel and realised we wouldn't have to pack up everything again the next morning, or in fact for a whole week.)

We learned very quickly that Glasgow railways are very much like the commuter networks in London, and perhaps this is why we felt so quickly at home. This and our new-found friend from Twitter, Kirsty, who showed us around and provided us with a gift basket of Irn-Bru and Tunnock's (since when we've been increasingly addicted to their teacakes). Over a very tasty pizza one night (followed by a Tunnock's dessert, obvs), Kirsty gave us a brief history of the industry in Glasgow. 'Edinburgh may have all the money,' she said, 'but yer Glasgow here's got all the bloody hard grafters.'

Left | Glasgow Subway, where the direction of travel is clockwise or anti-clockwise on either the inner or outer circle.

In the eighteenth century, Glasgow's success as a port – bringing in raw materials, exporting goods and transporting items on for further manufacture – was the envy of many other cities around the country. (The need to accommodate more and larger ships led to the development of Port Glasgow – now with its own train station about 20 miles outside Glasgow city centre.) Indeed, there doesn't seem to be an industry that didn't at one time or another find a place in the city. Engineering, shipbuilding, locomotive production, textiles, potteries, distilleries, tobacco products and clothing. You name it, Glasgow has likely done it. In the nineteenth century, as Glasgow's population exceeded even that of Edinburgh, its multiplying industries gave life to the sprawling suburbs which are now served by what we believe to be the second largest commuter rail network in Britain.

During our weekend off, we decided to go for a proper explore. Geoff took a complete circuit on the Subway, getting out at *all* 15 stops to say that he'd been to them all properly. The Subway is a great mini underground service, very easy to navigate and with oodles of character. Vicki in contrast set off to Uddingston to check out the incredible Tunnock's Tea Rooms and Bakery.

Vicki: While the tea rooms have a hint of nostalgia, the bakery looks like a regular factory. Albeit with a couple of pretty cool Tunnock's signs attached. They do tours, but they're super popular and get booked up well in advance, so sadly no luck for me on this occasion.

The sun didn't set until past eight each evening, and there was a glorious moment midweek when we found ourselves walking down West Nile Street, just to the west of the city centre. We hadn't realised that this part of the city is laid out in a square 'grid' system, similar to so many cities you see in America. As we crossed the road, the street to our left undulated mainly up, and the street to our right undulated down. The setting sun was spraying its golden rays and casting long shadows, and we both had flashbacks to a holiday in San Francisco (itself a beautiful city) the previous year – suddenly it felt like we were on the other side of the Atlantic. Glasgow was San Francisco, but better! Because it had more trains and a subway system, and is a lot easier to get to from home, which is why we know at some point we'll be making a return journey. *Geoff: During which I'll be making a 'Secrets of the Glasgow Subway' video.*

Opposite | Glasgow or San Francisco, you decide.

'Glasgow was San Francisco, but better!'

All The Castles

Britain's landscape is dominated by castles, and if it had been up to Vicki castles would have featured even more heavily in our adventure than they already do. Vicki's fascination started early in the journey, on day two in fact, when we made a quick visit to Pendennis Castle in Falmouth. When asked why she likes castles so much Vicki describes her 'respect for the ingenuity of people from the past. Who, without technology or mechanical machinery, refined a system of attack and defence that was in some instances impenetrable.'

The delicate art of warfare aside, castles are deeply rooted not just in the landscape, but in the fabric of society. Their stories lay the foundations of country and county borders, towns and cities, which later forged the positioning and routes of the railways we travel on today. The politics surrounding every castle – who owned it, who lived there, who visited, who inherited it, who was imprisoned there, which castles are still structurally intact, which ones are ruins – tells a much broader story than the physical buildings alone; a parallel

Above | To the castles!

that can again be drawn with the operation of the railways (not that we're saying anyone has ever been imprisoned on the railways, that we know of). It is for this reason that castles became much more than just an occasional feature of our adventure. And so, as hard as it was to choose, here are our top three castles we feel are more than just impressive fortifications.

Harlech

The walk to Harlech Castle from the station is a *very* steep climb. Thankfully, we have become quite expert at rushing up a gradient, mainly due to all the stairs and passenger bridges we've had to run over to make tight connections.

The castle, situated on the coast of north-west Wales, was built at the behest of King Edward I in the thirteenth century, following the death of Llywelyn ap Gruffudd (sometimes known as the last Welsh prince) in a battle against English forces near Builth.

Llywelyn's death was yet another milestone in a legacy of ongoing struggles to control Welsh lands that continued for many hundreds of years to come. This time the castle and surrounding area in Harlech remained in the hands of the English until the fifteenth century, when Owain Glyn Dwr led a revolt against English rule. Legend states that following his victory Harlech was the location for Owain's coronation as the new Prince of Wales. However, by 1409 – just five years later – Harlech was once again back under English control. In the centuries that followed, Harlech through rule and in law was considered part of England, along with the rest of Wales, although the two lands were never formally united under one name and the people of Wales would, we imagine, never have really considered themselves English. Nonetheless, the castle went on to play a significant role in many of what are always described as 'English' events. It was the capture of Harlech Castle, for example, by English Parliamentary troops which marked the end of the first stage of the English Civil War.

The use of the word 'English' to describe events that happened in Wales was really brought to light for us by the history we discovered at Harlech. For the first time, we began to consider the English-centric nature of Britain, and that while we would both consider ourselves to be part of the 'United Kingdom' we actually know next to nothing about either Welsh history or modern culture. We suddenly became much more aware of when one of us said English, when what we actually meant was British or, even more embarrassingly, Welsh.

It was with this realisation that we saw the importance of the railways, not just for travel in and of itself, but to gain new perspectives. To understand the different cultural connections – not just timetable connections – between different parts of the country.

> 'We suddenly became much more aware of when one of us said English, when what we actually meant was British or, even more embarrassingly, Welsh'

The use of the Welsh language is another great example of this. We made many attempts at picking up some Welsh words and phrases, and it gave us a great opportunity to chat with people, to find out more about local areas, understand why places are named in certain ways, and it gave us an insight into Welsh culture that no English translation could ever do. When we wanted to create some Welsh *All The Stations* t-shirts, we must have talked to at least ten different Welsh speakers and they all gave us a different way to say it! None of which we discovered were incorrect – it was just that everyone felt passionately that their phrasing was more accurate than the person we had spoken to before them. This taught us about the incredible diversity of expression of the Welsh language, of the passion of the Welsh people themselves and of the geographic boundaries between different parts of Wales where certain ways of speaking evolved separately from others – something we would never have discovered by speaking English alone.

Below | Harlech – is there a better-defended station on the network?

Harlech

Rochester

'Oozing with wonderful stories'

A prominent town since before Roman times, Rochester is oozing with wonderful stories. The history here is so thickly layered that, as you walk along the cobbled streets and around the ramshackle buildings, it is difficult to distinguish one time period from another, or to clearly understand the significance of the different events that have taken place. You certainly need to visit more than once.

Today it is perhaps most famous for its connection to Charles Dickens, who based multiple characters and locations on places in Rochester, many of which can still be seen today.

Of all the points of interest, however, we were drawn to the castle. Built not long after the Norman invasion of England in 1066, it was constructed in conjunction with eight others – Hertford, Berkhamsted, Windsor, Guildford, Reigate, Tonbridge, Rayleigh and Ongar – forming a defensive ring around London. The encircling castles were strategically placed 20 to 25 miles apart, so that if one should come under attack reinforcements could arrive from an adjacent stronghold within 24 hours. *Vicki: Another example of the pure genius of castles!*

Being of such importance, it is not surprising that Rochester Castle has been the scene of one or two battles. It endured its most famous siege in October 1215 when it was attacked by England's very own King John. The battle was fought against rebel barons and was connected to one of the most significant moments in English political history, the signing and subsequent annulment of the Magna Carta.

Below | Rochester Castle and Cathedral as seen from Rochester station.

Ironically, the barons used the strategic positioning of Rochester to prevent the king reaching London. After 40 days of fierce warfare, Rochester was eventually reclaimed by John.

The castle today is a shell of its former self, with only a few internal rooms surviving. But its position as a main thoroughfare to London is still echoed by the railways, with all main routes in Kent running through the town. Fortunately, you'd be very unlucky to be delayed by 40 days when passing through now.

Stirling

From the station, Stirling Castle is a good 20 minutes on foot through the town and up to the top of the hill. The climb is worth the effort as it is situated atop an old volcanic crag with panoramic views of the surrounding countryside – an awe-inspiring sight. Immediately adjacent to the castle is the Church of the Holy Rude, which includes an extensive graveyard full of elaborately carved memorials. We spent several minutes just absorbing the landscape – you would be hard pushed to find a more imposing or more Scottish-feeling location. *Vicki: Stirling satisfies all your imagined Scottish landscapes. Undulating crags, winding cobbled streets, men in kilts, Gothic mystery, blustering hillsides and even processioning bagpipers!*

> 'You would be hard pushed to find a more imposing or more Scottish-feeling location'

Like Rochester, there is an enormous sense of history, culture and tradition exuding from every corner of Stirling. Unlike Rochester, we recognised – as we had done in Wales – that Stirling's story was unfamiliar to us. It felt both fascinating and unsettling to look up at the statue of Robert the Bruce just outside the castle walls, to understand the name but to have no real idea of his significance. To rectify this, we popped into the castle gift shop to pick up a couple of quick guide books. Top tip: we often go for the children's guide – they are way more engaging and get you quickly to the best facts (instead of well-illustrated, but usually complicated, timelines).

We discovered that, since the twelfth century, Stirling has been at the hub of many key moments in Scottish history: battles, political struggles, royal births and even murder. When guide books talk about 'key moments' it can sometimes feel insincere, a phrase used to 'sell' the story of the attraction. Not so with Stirling, which was naturally important due to its strategically defensive position along the River Forth.

However, it is the events of the First War of Scottish Independence that stand out the most. In particular, the Battle of Bannockburn (an area named after the Bannock Burn, a river just a mile or so south of the city), in which Scottish troops led by Robert the Bruce defeated the significantly larger English army of Edward II. By reclaiming Stirling Castle this victory gave heart to Scottish forces and propelled other victories against the English in following years, leading eventually to the signing of the Declaration of Arbroath (which we later saw depicted on the platforms at Arbroath station, see chapter 6).

Above | Stirling Castle. It's almost impossible to take in the whole expanse of the landscape. We feel like no photograph will ever do it justice.

The Declaration sought acknowledgement from the Pope that Scotland was an independent country and Robert the Bruce their rightful king. While at the time the Declaration was not successful, it formed the basis of a later document, the Treaty of Edinburgh–Northampton, when Edward II finally acknowledged (in exchange for a significant amount of money, of course!) the independent status of Scotland and the ruling power of Robert the Bruce, now Robert I.

Even though these events are in the past, their impact is still evident today in the way modern Britain is divided geographically, socially and politically; in how areas are administered, talked about and lived in. In turn, these definitions are mirrored by the railways themselves, which follow the routes, boundaries and connections that were formed in some cases hundreds of years ago.

In contrast to Pilning station in Gloucestershire, which is still fighting for services, the line from Stirling to Alloa reopened in 2008 and exceeded all expectations, so much so that they have recently increased the number of services it provides. In 2016/17 more than 360,000 passengers arrived and departed from Alloa station, where previously passengers had to find alternative routes, or not, to make connections with Glasgow, Perth, Edinburgh, York and even London. The power of rail lines to reinforce the importance of some areas over others, and to bring new opportunities where previously none existed, is similar to the impact of castles centuries before, around which towns and industries would grow where previously there had been little or nothing.

Vicki's top ten castles in walking distance from stations

1 Conwy – 0.2 miles
2 Newark Castle – 0.3 miles
3 Harlech – 0.3 miles (uphill)
4 Rochester – 0.3 miles (pictured below)
5 Windsor – 0.3 miles (both Central and Riverside stations; Central is less hilly)
6 Caerphilly – 0.5 miles
7 Norwich – 0.5 miles
8 Pendennis – 0.7 miles (uphill)
9 Stirling – 0.8 miles (uphill)
10 Dover – 1.1 miles (uphill)

Best seaside towns near stations

1 St Ives – for art and tranquillity
2 Whitby – for literature and good fish & chips
3 North Berwick – for a warm welcome and wildlife
4 Saltburn – for the pier and knitting
5 Scarborough – for the cliff tramway (and castle)
6 Walton-on-the-Naze – for a picture-postcard view
7 Margate – for nostalgic streets
8 Barry Island – for Barrybados
9 Largs – for ice cream and Vikings
10 Skegness – for amusements

CHAPTER

REMEMBER TO GET OFF AT THE RIGHT STATION

REMEMBER TO GET OFF AT THE RIGHT STATION

Stations are at the heart of Britain's rail network and they were also at the heart of our journey. Each has its own significance, from the remote and desolate to the opulent and imposing. They encompass all aspects of a journey: for some they are meeting points, to others a point of passing. Some are cultural landmarks boasting architectural triumphs celebrating local craftsmanship; some are lost into urban or rural oblivion.

The unrelenting contrasts between and the specificities of each station are an endless source of fascination. Ardwick station, for example, opened in 1842 and is located just one stop outside of Manchester Piccadilly station. Despite its 175-year existence, when we visited, local people unanimously had never heard of it. A security guard who

Opposite | Short platforms like this one at Spooner Row are frequent features at request stops. Better make sure you're in the right carriage.

Right | Llanwrtyd Wells station on the Heart of Wales line, loved and cared for by the local community.

by his own admission has worked for 18 years just 150 metres away from the station entrance told us, 'Nah, you want Manchester Piccadilly, no such station here.' In 2016/17 Manchester Piccadilly welcomed 27.8 million people, while Ardwick saw just 860 passengers. The contrast could not be more staggering.

But stations aren't just places to catch trains. For many they are the centre of their community, providing opportunities for friendship and learning. Llanwrtyd Wells on the Heart of Wales line has a Station Friends group, a force of just six people (Llanwrtyd Wells is the smallest town in Britain) plus the local reverend who also helps out by cutting the grass. The group was formed independently 20 years ago, because they saw a need to make the station more appealing and easier to access for both the community and those visiting – when they began the platforms were covered in metre-high weeds. Ainslie, who heads up the group, works hard to get support and funding and as a result the station has won many awards for its flowers and gardens. They are volunteers, with no affiliations to any of the train operating companies. Just local people who see the importance and benefit the railways bring and who feel passionately that they want to maintain the level of service they have now for future generations.

We found that station staff have many ways of connecting with their communities. At Felixstowe, the mayor recently unveiled a new station mural created by young people from a nearby school. It's a scheme that has been running for over ten years and helps to make the station a place locals can be proud of. Meridian Water is a brand-new station

Above | Manchester Piccadilly, a vast and imposing station with surprisingly ornate details.

being built in north London (due to open in 2019). Here they're taking things a step further and creating a whole new community, including a school, thousands of homes and open park lands all positioned *around* the station.

Even stations that typically have more of a commuter community often find ways to connect with their passengers. Book swaps are very popular in lots of stations across the country. Acton Central (on the London Overground in west London) has a very well-stocked selection of books for people to take, read and return. Making us wonder, why not just go the whole hog and actually build a library into the station itself? You could catch the train directly *to* the library and make it a day out. With more and more public libraries closing, this could be a great way to solve the problem. Seriously, we're writing this one down – oh!

Whether large or small, stations form the basis of people's relationship with the railways. They are where we start and end our journeys. Passengers feel connected to their local station in different ways and, whether that station sees millions or tens of people every year, its importance to those who use it is paramount, and ultimately difficult to quantify. Needless to say, we believe there should be more stations and more trains to service them.

On our journey, we went to All The Stations. ('*All the stations, all of them*' as the lyrics in our theme tune went.) We *stopped* at every single station in Great Britain; we didn't, however, alight everywhere. There were some very practical reasons for this. Primarily it was a maths thing. To alight at all 2,563 stations and then wait to catch the next train would have taken about ten months – in some cases the 'next train' is not for another week. So instead, to say we had successfully visited a station the rule was that we had to be on the stopping train (the ones you try to avoid when making a long trip) that pulls into the station and allows passengers on and off. Wherever we could (sometimes the trains might be too busy, or we would be in the middle of interviewing someone) we took a few seconds on the platform to capture footage or a photograph.

'What about request stops?' we hear you cry. Well, yes, request stops were a little trickier to fathom out, they had a special rule. As of 2018 there are 147 request stops in the country, they are served infrequently and there is no guarantee that someone will ask for the driver to stop, even if the train is scheduled to do so. If we'd have asked to alight at every request stop in the schedule but didn't get off at any, we would have made ourselves very unpopular with the train crew. Therefore, we decided instead that we had to be *on* a train that was *scheduled* to stop, but even if it didn't we would still be able to count that as a 'visit'.

Geoff: In many cases when the train guards figured out what we were doing, and if the train wouldn't be delayed in the process, they often requested the driver to stop for us anyway. The Greater Anglia guard between Ely and Norwich, for example, gave us a few seconds at Spooner Row, just enough time to capture a couple of pics.

We visited 2,563 stations – but you don't need to go that far! Even if your journey only incorporates a handful of stations, you can still experience the various ways they serve and are served by their local community, both in the past and today. This chapter shares with you some of the greatest, the bizarre and quaintest stations that we encountered along our way.

Corrour – An Coire Odhar

'Choose Corrour'

We knew Corrour was going to be remote, although the word remote doesn't really do it justice. In 2010 Corrour featured in the BBC travel programme *Secret Britain* with Matt Baker, and the line they used to describe it was, 'It redefines the middle of nowhere.' We concur. Vehemently. The station is not accessible by any public roads – the nearest is about a ten-mile hike away.

Situated on a private estate at the edge of Rannoch Moor, Corrour station is made up of a platform, a passing loop (an additional section of line along a single-track route that allows trains travelling in the opposite direction to pass if required), a siding and a signal box, which has now been converted into rentable accommodation bookable via Airbnb. To the side of the tracks is the Station House, now a café, restaurant and mini shop, open from 8.30 a.m. until 9 p.m., serving wonderful food and drinks. The staff are predominately students employed seasonally. When we were there the lovely David was on duty, who chatted to us about the different aspects of working at the station. Due to its remoteness everyone lives on-site for the whole season (accommodation is available April–October only), and if they want to go somewhere other than the estate on their days off, there is no option but to catch the train.

Despite the remote location, we were surprised to see quite substantial numbers of people getting on and off the trains. Where was everyone going? We chatted to a couple in the café who told us they were just about to set off hiking across the moor to spend a night in a bothy. 'A what now?' we asked with a raise of our eyebrows. A bothy. Which we learnt is a small, very basic building, 'a wee house' the couple told us, four walls and not much more. You find them in remote parts of the country, they're quite prevalent in Scotland, and they are always open and free to stay in – though don't expect any facilities. It's a bring your own everything kind of situation, camping without a tent.

Another sign of the popularity of the area was a conversation Vicki had with a man and his dog. Nothing unusual about that you might think, but he was also carrying a spade (the man not the dog, that *would* have been weird). Vicki learnt that he was surveying for a large mobile phone company, to look at the viability of installing a phone mast in the area. The spade was to dig up soil samples to understand if building was practical.

Over the last two years Corrour has recorded the arrival and departure of just over 11,000 passengers annually, and whether for walking or the railways, the delights of the area keep bringing people back. Like ourselves – we've already returned to Corrour and noted that since our All The Stations journey there have been several new facilities added to the station platform. An electronic passenger information display has been installed, as well as a Caledonian Sleeper information point, complete with Wi-Fi (though the range is somewhat restricted).

Below | Corrour station makes an impressive landscape on the wilds of Rannoch Moor.

Speaking of trainspotting, another reason for people's interest in the station is its connection to one of the most recognisable scenes from the movie: *Trainspotting*. The classic shot of Ewan McGregor, Jonny Lee Miller, Ewen Bremner and Kevin McKidd standing on the platform as the train rolls away was one of our reasons for wanting to stop here. We of course had to recreate it.

Vicki: A word of warning if you've not seen Trainspotting. *Despite the title, it has little if nothing to do with trains. I was not prepared.*

Above | Corrour-spotting. Getting into character during our recreation of the iconic scene from *Trainspotting*.

And if *all* that wasn't enough of an allure, we accidentally discovered another little-known reason why some people might take a trip up to the wilds of the Scottish Highlands. If you're an aviation enthusiast this could be one for you. On the evening of our arrival Geoff suddenly cried, 'Can you hear that!' Instinctively our heads leant back at quite a sharp angle as the noise got louder and louder, until a four-propeller transporter plane flew directly above our heads. And we mean literally no more than 100 feet from the ground. 'Woah!' we both cried. 'Why aren't you filming!' Vicki yelled.

Back at the lodge David explained that it is a semi-regular occurrence due to the nearby RAF base. Pilots take the opportunity to practise flying low under the radar – an essential, if not sneaky, combat skill.

Far from the complete solitude and isolation we were expecting, Corrour was at times a mini hive of activity. Passengers arrive in crowds and then quickly disperse into the moor, like wisps of fog rolling mystically out of sight in the morning sunlight, leaving behind nothing but the wind whispering through the trees and over the tracks.

This felt a little bit like us on the morning of our departure as we flagged down the 8.58 a.m. sleeper train when it came clinking towards the station (incidentally the sleeper train is the only service you have to request to stop, all other trains are scheduled to alight). As we climbed up into the guard's compartment, the door slammed shut behind us and the driver pulled away, and just like that, Corrour was gone.

Coombe
Junction Halt

Coombe Junction Halt is a request stop station, one of only 147 on the network. Those of us who live in busy commuter cities are well versed at flagging down a bus, but flagging down a train is a whole different kind of experience. At a request stop the train will *only* stop if time-tabled to do so AND if it has been requested by a passenger. If you are on the train, all you have to do is tell the guard and they will con-tact the driver. If you're on the platform, it's very important that you 'make your intent clear'. We heard many stories of drivers not stopping because passengers didn't signal clearly enough that they wanted to board, and if you don't manage to get it to stop, it will probably be a good few hours until the next one. Our preferred method of flagging down a train is to hold out your arm at shoulder height, and maybe give a little wave too.

Above | The main line railway crosses the Looe Valley line on a viaduct, a clear illustration of the height difference between the main line and the branch line to Looe.

There is almost no greater pleasure in life than catching a train from a request stop, especially if the driver gives you a toot on the horn to let you know they've seen you. Joy!

Coombe Junction Halt is the first station after Liskeard on the Looe Valley branch line in Cornwall. Liskeard and Coombe weren't always connected; they sat adjacent to each other, approximately a mile apart on separate lines. Coombe was on the line from Looe, which originally carried goods to and from Bodmin Moor. Liskeard was on the main Great Western Railway route across Cornwall. When the business of transporting passengers became greater than goods, it was decided that the Looe Branch could be diverted up to Liskeard from Coombe station. As it turns out, that was easier said than done, because the hill is staggeringly steep. But if history has taught us anything it's that the Victorians did not let something as trivial as gravity stand in the way of expanding their rail network. Coombe was no exception; they simply built the track in a wide sweeping curve, creating the flattest route possible.

What this means, though, is that when departing Coombe Junction Halt the driver has to reverse out. To do this is a two-person job. While the driver switches ends, the guard jumps out, walks a few feet along the track and disappears into a tiny wooden hut, inside which is the ground frame and, hopefully on cold mornings, a cup of tea. The guard switches the ground frame (just a fancy name for a lever) to move the track points so that the train can continue either down to Looe or back up to Liskeard, depending on the direction of travel. We saw a few families craning their heads, as we were, to catch a glimpse of this unique manoeuvre. In a world of automated signalling, GPS and Netflix on demand in your pocket, witnessing such a manual operation is somehow inexplicably brilliant.

Very few people ever get on or off at Coombe. In fact, when we visited it was the second least-used station in the whole of the country, with only 48 recorded passengers in 2015/16. Maybe because of this, or maybe because of its isolated location, we decided that at least one of us needed to board by flagging down the train. On the morning of our visit Vicki drew the short straw and ended up travelling on the train from Liskeard while Geoff got to take the scenic route and walk down the road, which then became a quiet country lane, past a farm, past a field, down the hill, through a wooden swing gate, along the track-side path and onto the lonely solitary platform of the station.

Above | Ground frame boxes at Coombe Junction Halt.

Geoff: It was totally calm and unforgettably peaceful at the station. There was maybe a slight breeze, in the distance I could hear a stream babbling, birds singing and then the familiar sound of a diesel engine. The trackbed did that thing where it whistled with the hum of a motive unit and then from behind the cover of the trees came a set of headlights and the one-car train trundled over the points and pulled slowly in.

It seemed surreal that a train would run here at all. We couldn't help but look at our watches and think about how a couple of hundred miles away in, say, south-east London or suburban Greater Manchester, thousands of passengers would be piling into their morning commute, squeezing into every available cubic centimetre of space on the platform of their local station. While at the same time, as the guard casually switched the points and climbed back up into the train, the Liskeard to Looe train clattered back over the points, now set to follow the shoreline of the East Looe River all the way to the coast.

We also need to give a shout-out to walking group Plymouth – Walks with History, who as a result of our trip to Coombe have started organising regular trips to the station, to explore to the local area but also to boost passenger numbers. Fingers crossed for the 2017/2018 passenger statistics!

Worcester Shrub Hill

We now say that it was fate that took us to Shrub Hill, because we certainly hadn't been planning to alight there. We *had* been hoping to focus our attention on Great Malvern station, but the Finstock Flyer sadly put paid to that. The 'Finstock Flyer' is the name, told to us by platform staff at Oxford station, that they give to the evening service from London Paddington to Great Malvern. After Oxford, it stops at Combe, Finstock and Ascott-under-Wychwood, stations that only get two services a day, one in the morning and the Flyer in the evening.

The day we caught the Flyer (incidentally, the alternative title to Ocean Colour Scene's classic hit), it was already running about 20 minutes late when we boarded at Oxford. That doesn't sound like a lot, but the other thing you should know about the Finstock Flyer is that between Oxford and Great Malvern a lot of the service runs on a single not double-track line.

This was one of the things we found frustrating about being delayed here, and something that people often forget when talking about the disadvantages of Dr Beeching's railway closures. Beeching's 1963 report 'The Reshaping of British Railways' not only proposed to close entire lines and stations to save money, but also to turn double-track lines into single tracks to reduce the cost of maintenance and upkeep.

'Did the Victorians have these kinds of problems!?'

The downside today is that if there is a fault or a blockage with the line then it affects services in both directions rather than just one. And not only is this exactly what happened to us, we were also caught by a points failure just outside of Shrub Hill station itself.

Geoff: It was probably the points failure that annoyed me the most. Despite being 2017 it seems we still can't engineer a set of points that don't melt in the heat! I couldn't help but wonder: did the Victorians have these kinds of problems!?

We were unprepared, and distracted by the impending fear that we might be stuck on a rail replacement bus for the next two hours. But even so the delights of Shrub Hill could not fail to grab our attention. The longer we were there the more we were pleased to have been delayed.

The first thing to note is the incredible disc semaphore signalling on Platform 1. Historically disc signals like this were used where there was limited physical space for infrastructure. At Shrub Hill they are

Above | Worcester Shrub Hill boasts what we believe to be the last working example of platform disc signalling on the network.

situated underneath the platform canopy, so a more traditional 'long-armed' semaphore would have been impractical. Thought to be the last of their kind in use on the network, their current purpose is to help increase the service capacity of the station by splitting the platform in two as needed, creating A and B ends for multiple services to arrive on the platform at the same time. While efficient for train scheduling, split platforms can be confusing for passengers – especially if you are unfamiliar, as we were, with a station. 'Where does 2a finish and 2b begin?' 'Are we standing in the right place?'

The smaller signal (the one with the letters CO) is the 'Calling On' signal that indicates that a train can move along the platform once the opposite end is clear.

The most notable feature of the station is the restored ladies waiting room on Platform 2. The room has an iron frame, which was cast by the Vulcan Iron Works, located just a stone's throw from Shrub Hill. Its ceramic tiles were manufactured by Maw & Co, originally a Worcester-based company. The varying patterns used in the tiling, together with the unique frame, has led experts to believe that this was a prototype.

Perhaps an example of local companies working together to generate their own business opportunities? In fact, after the installation of the waiting rooms at Shrub Hill, Maw & Co became a major contractor for the railways, right up until the mid-twentieth century when the need for station tiling made a sudden plummet (Beeching *cough*).

The tiles are the stand-out feature of the room. The purple, white and green detail reminded us of the suffragette campaign colours and triggered a memory of reading about the waiting room in one of the only published books about women on the railways we could find. In *Railwaywomen*, Helena Wojtczak describes how 'At Worcester, GWR, in 1873 Ladies' Attendant Mrs Dale earned 10s'. The book lists salaries of other staff at Worcester and in comparison to other stations, illustrating the disparity between like jobs and between men and women, an issue which is still relevant today, and not just on the railways.

Shrub Hill is a crucial junction for trains travelling across the West Midlands. Destinations include Hereford, Malvern, Birmingham, London, Bristol and Oxford. Given the volume of traffic we were surprised by the fact that a single-track system is still in place, that there aren't more platforms at the station and that the signalling systems are so quaint. Obviously, we love a quaint station, but we wonder if Shrub Hill might be in need of an upgrade to help cope with today's commuting demands, particularly when things go a little awry in the heat.

This is not, however, a reason to avoid making a trip here, as we unexpectedly discovered – the delights of the station far outweighed our frustration at being held up.

Below | The ladies waiting room is a Grade II listed building, renovated by Network Rail and the Railway Heritage Trust.

Shippea Hill

'There's no one here'

If there's one station that's probably had more than its fair share of publicity in recent times, then it's Shippea Hill in Cambridgeshire. On the line between Ely and Norwich, just outside the Norfolk boundary, it is a request stop and has an obscure service, just one train in one direction weekday mornings – meaning that you can't return. On a Saturday there is an increased service. You can leave on the morning train and return early evening. Party time, but not too late, in Norwich!

When we visited Shippea Hill, according to the 2015/16 statistics from the Office of Rail and Road, it was officially Britain's least-used station. Only 12 people had used it the *entire year* (that's just one person per month). This was clearly a station that did not see a lot of passengers. It had a boost on Christmas Eve 2016 when *Bake Off* finalist Ian Cumming offered free mince pies to anyone who got off the train there. This lured 16 people to all be there at the same time. We figured we could beat this! So as soon as we started planning our adventure we marked 'Shippea Hill Day' as a chance to do something a little different.

We put a call out to those we considered our most adventurous friends and acquaintances, to see who might be up for catching a

Below | Looking east; Shippea Hill, Britain's least-used station 2015/16.

7.25 a.m. train from the middle of the Cambridgeshire countryside just for the hell of it. You know you have chosen your friends well when, in response to such an absurd request, no one questions your sanity. Instead they replied with either a vigorous 'See you there!', a frustrated 'Ah I'm already doing something' or a tentative 'Let me see if I can get out of work'.

Some drove up from London on the day, which meant they started driving at 5 a.m. Others, like us, travelled down the night before, and we all booked ourselves into the closest Travelodge we could find. With a whole evening to ourselves, we did what any self-respecting group of railway enthusiasts would do – we ordered pizza, played cards and chatted trains.

However they got there, at just after 7 a.m. on Saturday 3 June 2017 there were a total of 21 people waiting to flag down the train on the eastbound platform of Shippea Hill station. What we didn't expect was the addition of three local ladies from the nearby village. Actual passengers! I think we were as surprised to see them as they were to see us. The ladies turned out be supporters of the Shippea Hill Station Society and were also on a mission to boost passenger numbers. Their plan for the day was to take the morning train, enjoy some shopping and lunch in Norwich before returning on the evening service. This was the second trip they had made that year and they hoped that their efforts, along with other local supporters, would prevent further cuts to the service.

Below | Looking west; Shippea Hill station has just one shelter for its two platforms, a help point and a disused signal box.

Right | Twenty-four passengers making their intent clear. (Photo by Roger Newark.)

As the train drew near we created perhaps one of the best photos of our entire trip. The sight of 24 people (arranged in height order) holding out their arms to 'make their intent clear' and request the driver to stop and let us all on. (We even got a toot from the driver – perfect!)

Once on the train the journey was plain sailing and we reached Norwich with enough time for a local pub breakfast before we all got the train back to Ely an hour later. This time we stopped at Lakenheath (another request stop), which we couldn't tick off on the way out. Bizarrely, because of the stopping patterns between Shippea Hill and Lakenheath it is never actually possible to travel between these two stations on the same train, even though they are just one stop up the line from each other.

With such a lack of passengers we started to consider whether, if the line between Ely and Norwich was being built today, Shippea Hill would even get a station. Back in the heyday of Victorian railway madness stations were built all over the place; even the smallest of hamlets got its own stop. At the time, very few people had their own private mode of transport and journeys by road were long and uncomfortable. For those in isolated communities like Shippea Hill the coming of the railways brought an opportunity for travel never even dreamed of before. Today, with the popularity of car ownership, it could be argued that Shippea Hill might not 'need' a station, but there are clearly 12 people a year who use it and it would be shame if it didn't have one – why else might you make a trip into the wilds of the Cambridgeshire countryside?

All The Family History

The notion that Shippea Hill would signify a special stage in our journey was amplified when Vicki discovered a personal connection.

The first time Vicki had any idea there might be some railway blood in her family was in February 2017, when her mum very casually mentioned one evening, 'Oh, you know my grandad worked on the railways.' 'Errr, no!' was Vicki's hasty reply. A few weeks later a handwritten family tree and some photographs not only confirmed Vicki's great-grandad had worked on the railways, but so had her great-great-grandad and her great-great-great-grandad, as well as various other members of the family. From signalmen to porters and even railway labourers, this revelation seemed to suggest that Vicki's family had not simply worked on the railway but had also perhaps had a hand, literally, in building or maintaining parts of it.

'Oh, you know my grandad worked on the railways'

Looking at the census records we saw that Vicki's great-grandad, William Wilby, worked as a signalman, and in 1901 he was boarding at Burnt Fen Station. A little more digging revealed that Shippea Hill has had many name changes over the years. When it opened in 1845 it was called Mildenhall Road, by 1885 it was known as Burnt Fen, finally becoming Shippea Hill in 1904.

But what did 'boarding at' mean? It implies Shippea Hill/Burnt Fen wasn't his normal place of work. Perhaps he travelled to various parts of the network to work where required? With the status of signalman, William would have been considered highly skilled and would have dealt with a significant amount of responsibility. The same as modern-day signallers, it's their job to make sure all the trains that pass their signal box do so safely.

It was and remains a lonely job. William would likely have worked almost completely alone, except for the sending and receiving of messages from other signallers further up or down the line. And somewhere like Shippea Hill, with nothing to see for miles around, must have increased that feeling of isolation. In his book *The Railways: Nation, Network & People*, Simon Bradley describes the life of a signalman as 'closer in some ways to the isolation of the lighthouse than to the companionship of the footplate or the ready exchanges of the station platform'.

Vicki: This was almost too much to really believe. Of all the stories that I thought we would end up hearing on this journey, I never thought they would be about my own family. It made me understand better how important the railway was to the livelihoods of so many people, particularly for those living outside of the big cities. They changed the prospects of whole families, just like mine, who prior to the railways would have worked as agricultural labourers, which was seasonal and unpredictable. I imagine there are lots of people with family connections to the network that they never knew existed. Might be worth a subscription to Ancestry, no? Go on!

Opposite | Back row, 3rd from the right. William Wilby, signalman at Shippea Hill and Vicki's great-grandad. Back row, 2nd from left. Herbert Wilby, William's son.

Below | Shippea Hill signal box where William would have worked. Thought to be the original, though with some modernised sections.

Smethwick Rolfe Street

Often the smaller stations reveal as much about the importance of the railways as the obvious network landmarks. A notable example of this is Smethwick Rolfe Street, located at the heart of suburban Smethwick in the West Midlands, but overshadowed by its larger, more impressive neighbour Birmingham New Street. New Street boasts 25 platforms and 33 escalators, while Rolfe Street has 2 platforms and just 2 staircases. But what Rolfe Street lacks in stature, it makes up for in its welcoming atmosphere and the opportunities it offers those who live and work within the local community.

We were invited to stop at Rolfe Street by Peter Chapman, then customer service assistant, and Faye Lambert, head of community rail for London Midland (now West Midland and London Northwestern Railway). It just so happened that the week we were due to arrive in Birmingham the station was preparing to unveil a new community artwork on the platforms. We were a few days early for the official launch, but nothing was too much trouble at Rolfe Street and we were still given the opportunity for a sneak preview; a chance to see the finishing touches of the artwork being installed and chat with the team who had made it all happen.

The theme of the project was 'Going Forward' with a focus on co-curation and representing the vibrancy and cultural diversity of Smethwick. Staff partnered with art students from nearby Sandwell College and public artist Steve Field, and the group spoke with local people to understand more about their experiences of living in the area, using the station and what messages they would like to see on display. The artwork combines artistic elements from all the students and shows a strong link to the area's history of cultural migration and community cohesion. The phrase 'Love thy neighbour' is repeated in multiple languages all spoken in the town, and at the centre of the piece are two hands planting seeds, symbolising the community working and growing together for the future.

'What Rolfe Street lacks in stature, it makes up for in its welcoming atmosphere'

The art commission is just one of three project elements. Construction students from Sandwell also got involved refurbishing the old station master's office, now a community exhibition space, and other groups came together to revive the station garden. These kinds of projects are important opportunities to see stations as more than just places where you can catch a train or pick up a timetable – rather as places that can offer something more: skills, experience, friendship, a pathway to work, a place to feel safe, get to know your neighbours and feel proud of where you live.

While we were at the station, passengers took time to stop, look and photograph the artwork, even though it wasn't finished. One lady said how positive it was, and how happy it made her feel to see her home language, Polish, represented.

Whenever you next stop at a station, look around. Is there any artwork on the platforms, flowers growing in a garden or any posters on display in the ticket hall? Think more about the people who may have come together to create it or look after it. Does it reflect the way you feel about the area, does it represent the people you know or live next door to? How could you get involved?

Above | The waiting room at Market Rasen, with artwork created by local young people and a plentiful book exchange.

Market Rasen

OK, we *have* to talk about Lincolnshire. Seriously, where did all the stations go? And come to that, the motorways too? Of all the areas on the rail network, Lincolnshire felt by far the most isolated and least connected of anywhere in the country, including the Scottish Highlands. Take a look at a map and you will see just two railway lines skirting around the top and bottom of the county. In the north the line runs from Lincoln round to Cleethorpes and in the south down to Skegness. But what do you do if you live in the middle, somewhere like Horncastle or Partney? *Vicki: More importantly, how would I ever get to Tattershall Castle?*

The answer is, of course, that most people in Lincolnshire will own a car. Though without any motorways this also feels like it might not be a quick or convenient way to get from place to place. We took a taxi from Market Rasen to Gainsborough (part of our plan to catch the Saturday-only Gainsborough Central service) and the journey along the A1103 was as narrow and winding as any B-road we've ever been down.*

*It was also quite dangerous. Another statistic about Lincolnshire: annually it has more road deaths than any other county in Great Britain. *Geoff: I sent a tweet to our followers indicating that if no one ever heard from us again, we were last seen in a taxi on the A1103.*

Above | A large, warm welcome at Market Rasen.

With stations across the county few and far between, our expectations were low with regard to facilities, points of interest or what we might find when we decided to stop at Market Rasen. We were, however, VERY pleasantly surprised.

Rather than neglected or underwhelming, Market Rasen was an absolute delight! The more we looked around the more we fell in love. There were no elaborate buildings, architectural innovations or famous railway associations, but instinctively it felt loved by its community and well cared for by the local Station Adoption Group, who had clearly spent lots of time and passion caring for the platforms, waiting rooms and gardens.

There was artwork and posters by local young people (some with the very sage advice, reminding travellers not to 'run on the track because you could slip and die'. Quite). There were blooming flower beds, a book exchange and an enormous 'Welcome' sign, something we didn't see anywhere else on the network.

A plaque by the entrance to the station invited us to explore more of the station's history, providing a QR link to the Market Rasen Heritage Tour website and a YouTube video with more information (you can also just Google it).

'Where did all the stations go?'

We learnt that the railway arrived in Market Rasen in 1848, and brought with it a plethora of new opportunities for the local population, for business and pleasure (and those wishing to attend the races). And while the service and connections today are more limited, it remains one of the essential ways for people to access other parts of the county, and country.

But let's do the maths. Today, it takes at best two-and-a-half hours to travel from Market Rasen to Skegness by rail, whereas in the car the journey is approximately one hour. Worse still, the 112 miles from Market Rasen to Birmingham takes three-and-a-half hours, which you could easily reduce to two hours by road.

We began to think about the impact of living somewhere with such awkward connections to public transport and realised that inevitably it mostly affects those who cannot afford a car, or those not able to drive one. We often focus on the importance of railways for adults, particularly commuters. But what about the opportunities for young people? If the options for independent travel are limited or frustratingly long (from places like Market Rasen it could take you longer to travel than the time you have available at your destination), it's easy to see how you might forgo public transport altogether.

And it's not just Lincolnshire where this is the case. In chapter one we mentioned Pilning station, which currently struggles with just two services a week in one direction, but there are many other awkwardly situated and lesser-served stations around the country. *Vicki: I grew up in an isolated area in Norfolk, and was always reliant on my parents to drive me to see friends, visit cities or access cultural venues. If there had been more train services or if some of the stations in my local area had never closed, I would have been able to travel more independently at a younger age, and so pursue broader interests. This may have changed my whole outlook.*

The care and attention given to Market Rasen by the Station Adoption Group shows the significance the railway still has for the local community, despite its limited services. The idea that more can be offered, to great effect, is something we feel passionately about. As a start, even just an increase in the number of carriages each service provides would make the journey more comfortable and encourage others to travel. We arrived on a very packed single-car unit, squished up against our fellow passengers, who told us through muffled armpits that this was very much the norm.

Knaresborough

'Despite appearances Knaresborough very much operates as a modern station'

Knaresborough is a quintessential Victorian railway station and it's brilliant! There, that's it, that's all you need to know. OK, well, seeing as we spent quite a bit of time there, here's some more of the details.

Located on the Harrogate line between Leeds and York, the first thing to notice (because you really can't miss it) is Knaresborough Viaduct. It is immediately to the west of the station and carries the railway across the River Nidd, and you really do have to crane your neck upwards to see it because it is a staggering 30 metres (approx. 100 feet) high. The close proximity of the viaduct to the station means that some of the track points are actually on top of the bridge itself, and terminating trains have to reverse back onto it in order to prepare to travel back the way they've come.

Below | Knaresborough viaduct.

The viaduct is a listed structure, along with the station itself, the signal box, the station water tower, the lamplighter's hut, and the south and north portals of the railway tunnel. On the westbound platform, heritage posters have been installed above what is probably one of the longest station benches in the country (although not *the* longest, that distinction falls to Scarborough with its incredible 139-metre-long – 456-foot – bench). As we said, quintessentially Victorian.

Yet, despite appearances, Knaresborough very much operates as a modern station. It is unstaffed, with tickets purchased by machine only, or on the train if they're not working. The dot matrix indicators and automated voice announcements are the only way passengers are kept up to date with any service alterations (unless you have an app). All the original station rooms, such as the ticket office, parcel office and waiting rooms, are now used for commercial purposes including a café (serving Yorkshire tea, of course) and, randomly, a picture framing business. Many of the rooms are currently unoccupied though, waiting for renovation, which as a listed building cannot be easy or cheap to do. There are some wonderful murals around the station including one of a ticket clerk in the station entrance, indicating where staff would have worked but have long since departed.

Below | The cheerful booking clerk has a Harry Potter feel about him!

The lack of human presence feels incongruous somehow. While we love the atmosphere of a more isolated location such as Coombe Junction or Shippea Hill, Knaresborough is far from remote. It is surrounded by houses and businesses and just a short walk from the town centre. On the day we were there, it was raining quite heavily and there was nowhere to shelter except the platforms themselves (the café was closed). A warm waiting room or ticket office would have brought an extra something to an otherwise beautiful station.

There are signs that a more human touch is returning. Friends of Knaresborough Station are very active and have recently made some wonderful additions to the platforms, including a rockery, trolley planters and a brilliant 'bug hotel' – a place for wildlife, not humans, to come and thrive!

OKEHAMPTON STATION

NO PARKING BY FOOTWAY

DOGS MUST BE KEPT ON LEADS

Above | Okehampton station
as you approach it on foot.
Chances are, if you arrive by
train, you may never exit this
side of the building.

Okehampton and Sampford Courtenay

At the end of each day that we travelled, we updated the map on our website to show where we had been – grey 'unvisited' blobs turned green as we 'ticked!' them off, and slowly the map changed colour. Three weeks into our journey we started to get a few comments saying, 'It looks like you've missed out two stations!' as sure enough, there were two grey blobs amongst a sea of green – those two stations were Okehampton and Sampford Courtenay in north-west Devon.

Situated on a branch off the Barnstaple Line, these stations remain two of the most unusual on the entire UK network. Passenger trains from Exeter operate here on a Sunday, but ONLY in the summer months (late May to September). So, while we'd visited every other Devonian station at the start of our trip in early May, we had to make

Above | Sampford Courtenay recorded just 144 passengers between 2016/17, making it Britain's 12th least-used station.

a return for just one day. That day turned out to be Sunday 25 June.

The stations were originally just two on a much longer line that continued west to Bude then south to Plymouth, but it was cut back to Okehampton in the 1960s due to, yes you guessed it, Dr Beeching. Further cuts in the 1970s saw both Okehampton and Sampford Courtenay lose their passenger services altogether.

Over the years the line remained active with freight from Meldon Quarry, so that when plans to reopen Okehampton station and run services along part of the original line were proposed they at least didn't have to start from scratch. The first summer Sunday services between Exeter and Okehampton started in 1997. Heritage operations between Okehampton and Meldon Viaduct began in the early 2000s.

The business and operational running of the line is complex. The impetus for reopening this section of the network came from a collaboration between Devon County Council, West Devon Borough Council and Dartmoor National Park with the aim of bringing tourism back to the area. Okehampton station, the track along the line and heritage services to Meldon Viaduct are looked after by Dartmoor

Railway, while the summer Sunday shuttle is provided by GWR (with financial support from the county council). Confused? Us too.

While this is an almost untangle-able web of invested organisations, the thing to note is that everyone involved continues to work tirelessly, against many competing constraints, to provide ongoing services to the public. In particular, Dartmoor Railway is what is known as a 'community interest company', an organisation defined by law as entirely focused on providing services for the public good. It is our impression that through their dedication as a business, but also the endless hours volunteered by their Supporters group, there continues to be an appetite to run a regular, albeit limited, service.

The work of Dartmoor Railway isn't just operational. As we travelled the line, we were approached by a gentleman with a clipboard (always an apprehensive moment) who was surveying passengers to find out where they had travelled from and where they were going to. The data collected was to campaign for the continuance of the existing service as well as the hope to increase it. Though, when we said we had started our journey from Penzance 49 days ago, we fear we may have skewed their statistics.

'Providing services for the public good'

One of the brilliant things you can witness along the line, if you're up early enough, is the guard on the first train of the day out of Exeter, who will alight at Sampford Courtenay to physically open the station and unlock the gates. On the last train of the day, the sequence is reversed and the guard makes sure the station is secured overnight. Despite being a summer Sunday service, in 2016/17 Sampford Courtenay welcomed around 144 passengers (we can sense Shippea Hill hanging its semaphore in shame).

Okehampton station itself is very pretty (or rather, very quaint) with loads of original station features: a museum, a station café (serving a great English breakfast – we can personally attest to that), Percy the friendly station cat who comes and says hello and, a railway-lover's dream, a shop that sells old second-hand railway paraphernalia.

Vicki: I lost Geoff while we were at Okehampton, and when I eventually found him in the station shop he looked at me sheepishly and the lady behind the counter laughed. I knew his backpack was going to be a few second-hand timetables heavier on our way home.

While there, we hopped onto a heritage train (it would have been rude not to) to take the short journey further west to Meldon. At Meldon you should prepare yourself for a not-so-small jaw-dropping

moment. Meldon Viaduct is a wrought-iron truss bridge that opened in 1874 and has dominated the landscape ever since. The line has now been turned into a cycle track which links up to the Granite Way trail. Sadly trains have not passed over the viaduct since the 1990s.

Since completing All The Stations, news has reached us that plans are now in place to trial a commuter service from Okehampton to Exeter; this includes the building of a brand-new station, Okehampton Parkway. To bring back a regular service to a line that was scrapped in its entirety is an incredible achievement. There is currently no timeline in place for when this new service might be operational, so for now you'll have to be content with taking a ride on one of the most unique services in the country – but don't hang around too long, remember it is summer Sundays only and we don't get too many of those!

Independent Stations

While not unusual to meet a station master (or mistress) when doing All The Stations, Alex, the then station master of Chester-le-Street station in County Durham, didn't work for any of the 27 train operating companies we had travelled with on our journey so far. Nor did he work for Network Rail, or the Rail Delivery Group or any other rail company we'd ever heard of. But Alex did manage a company rather cheekily called Chester-le-Track, and he owned and ran the ticket office at Chester-le-Street as well as another station down the line, Eaglescliffe.

Independently run ticket offices! Despite our obvious love and interest in the railways, we hadn't realised that such a phenomenon existed. Thankfully Alex was able to tell us more. In the 1990s, when the railways became privatised, business opportunities sprang up around the country to run ticket offices and other station facilities on the network. Not many people did it, but in 2017 there were still about 20 independently run stations across the country.

Some are managed by local authorities – Clitheroe and Carnforth ticket offices for example are operated on behalf of Lancashire County Council. Others, like Chester-le-Street, are operated by entirely separate organisations.

As well as looking after the ticket office some companies own other areas of the station building too. At Chester-le-Street Alex and his staff managed the waiting room and toilet facilities, and rented out some of the other rooms to local businesses – a taxi company and dance school were in situ during our visit. At Carnforth, much of the

'We hadn't realised such a phenomenon existed'

Independently run ticket offices

Aber	Gobowen	Newtown (Powys)
Bargoed	Ledbury	Pembrey & Burry
Barmouth	Leominster	Port
Bishop Auckland	Llandrindod Wells	Pengam
Burscough Bridge	Ludlow	Severn Tunnel
Carnforth	Milford Haven	Junction
Chepstow	Millom	Whitby
Clitheroe	Nelson	

Above | At Carnforth you can even dress up as *Brief Encounter* characters Laura Jesson and Alec Harvey.

building is occupied by the Carnforth Station Heritage Centre, owned and operated by the Carnforth Station and Railway Trust Company – another completely independent organisation. (Carnforth is perhaps unique due to its connection to the 1940s film *Brief Encounter*. The heritage centre is dedicated to the story of David Lean's classic romance – you can take tea in the recreated café, dress up as the lead characters and even watch the film in a screening room where it plays on a loop.)

Without the option to provide add-ons, such as a refreshment room or gift shop, or the ability to rent out spaces to other businesses, its a challenge to generate enough revenue from ticket sales alone. In fact, just a year after meeting Alex, we were saddened to hear that Chester-le-Track had stopped trading.

A large factor in the decline of independent ticket offices is the trend for purchasing tickets online. Less human interaction is required. For us, the idea of stations without people is genuinely upsetting. A large part of what makes the railways so great is the passion and dedication of the people who work there. It's the personal touch, which Alex told us he strove for as an independent company. And his staff were not just knowledgeable about tickets; they also attended on the platforms, making sure those who needed help got it, providing up-to-date information about services and just generally making the station a nicer place to be.

How often do you buy your tickets in person at a station? Is there a choice between tapping at a machine or chatting to someone at the counter? Do you even know who runs your local ticket office? You may think it's all part of the same wider national railway operations, but check the list opposite – it could be a very local business offering something slightly different.

Chances are, like us sometimes, you go for convenience over conversation. But what if just once a week you step up to the counter instead? You might discover a discount you never knew existed, or get help carrying your suitcase to the platform, or save 10 per cent on your next cup of tea in the café next door – something that makes your day and theirs a little bit better.

Wemyss Bay – Bàgh Nan Uaimhean

Everyone said, 'Just wait until you get to Wemyss Bay!' We couldn't, but first we had to learn how to pronounce it. It took us a while but eventually we managed to remember the emphasis (and Scottish lilt) on 'Weeeems' not *Whem-ess* (it was that silent 'y' sneaking in where it wasn't wanted which kept catching us out).

Weeeems Bay is beautiful. Yes, we know what you're thinking: stations are functional, impressive, grand and often quaint, but are they beautiful? Well yes, Wemyss Bay is. Its elegance is largely due to the incredible sweeping curve that runs through the entire structure of the building. A building which is not just a railway station, but also a ferry terminal. And here lies the secret to the whole thing.

The railway came to Wemyss Bay to join up with the popular Clyde steamers. Steamers began carrying passengers across the Firth of Clyde from Glasgow to a variety of locations in the early nineteenth century. Their popularity grew as the ever-increasing population of Glasgow sought day trips to escape the harsh urban landscapes of the city, and the railways wanted in on the action – much to the dismay of the steamers, who lost out on revenue once everyone realised taking the train could save them a considerable amount of time. The first Railway Pier, as it was known, at Wemyss Bay opened in 1865. By 1899 the Caledonian Railway (General Powers) Act laid out plans for the rebuild of both Wemyss Bay and Glasgow Central stations. Both would undergo phenomenal transformations, both designed by architect James Miller and the Caledonian Railway chief engineer Donald Matheson.

During our visit we were lucky enough to meet with Nancy Cameron, founder of the Friends of Wemyss Bay Station, who told us more about Matheson's design. Influenced heavily by a visit to Chicago, where Matheson had seen successful methods of crowd control implemented in public spaces, the design of the new Wemyss Bay station excluded the use of corners or right angles and used instead only curves. The purpose of which was to guide large numbers of passengers seamlessly from the train platforms to the ferry pier, and vice versa. There are no right angles restricting your view, no bottlenecks and no disappearing corridors to get lost down; the building itself guides you to exactly where you need to go quickly and efficiently. Even the urinals in the male toilets are on a curve, but whether or not this helps visitors to use them quickly or efficiently we cannot say.

Geoff: The station is both practical and aesthetically very pleasing, it wasn't often on our journey that we had seen those two features working so harmoniously together. Take Leeds for example, practical but not so easy on the eye. Sorry Leeds. (Not sorry.)

The most impressive thing about Wemyss Bay, however, is not the station architecture but the incredible book shop and café managed by the very dedicated Friends of Wemyss Bay Station. It is their care and attention to detail that transforms the station from a building of impressive architectural stature to one of beauty. The First Class Second Hand Book Shop and (recently opened) Gallery, housed in the original first class waiting rooms, offers a place for visitors and locals alike to meet, enjoy stories from the station's past and contribute to its future (all proceeds go towards the upkeep of the station). Hanging flowers are all grown by the Friends and bring not just a splash of colour to the building but also the delights of wildlife too – we spotted delicate cabbage white butterflies on their blooms.

But all this is almost irrelevant unless people actually use the station. In the past, hundreds of daily passengers disembarked from the train to connect with the ferry for their weekends away from the city. Does that still happen? In recent years the price of the ferry was disproportionately high and passenger footfall low. But the Scottish government, as part of plans to support isolated island communities, has provided subsidies to ferry companies. This has brought prices down in some cases by 35 per cent, which means more people can make the journey across the Clyde. The passenger usage numbers for the railway also reflect this, with an increase of almost 35,000 between 2015/16 and 2016/17, to more than 200,000. Of course, we can't tell if everyone using the train has caught the ferry, but observations by the Friends suggest that more and more people are.

This coming together of the Friends of Wemyss Bay with support from the government gives a glimpse of how a station can operate at its best and provide more than simply a building for the arrival or departure of trains. This is really what is most beautiful about Wemyss Bay.

Below | The picture-perfect flowers at Wemyss Bay are grown by the station Friends group.

'There are no right angles'

Vicki's quaint scale

Following Vicki's concerns that she might end up using the word 'quaint' quite a lot to describe stations that looked 'pretty and historical', with the help of our project followers we established the idea of a 'quaint scale'. There were lots of attempts on Twitter and Facebook to create a graphic illustration explaining the scale, but none were officially adopted. We are excited therefore to reveal for the first time Vicki's official quaint scale guide to railway stations. Ta-da!

Vicki: I hope this guide will help my fellow adventurers measure the levels of quaint throughout their journeys. As a guide, think of Redcar British Steel as a 1, with somewhere like Market Rasen a solid 5 and Appleby an incontrovertible 10.

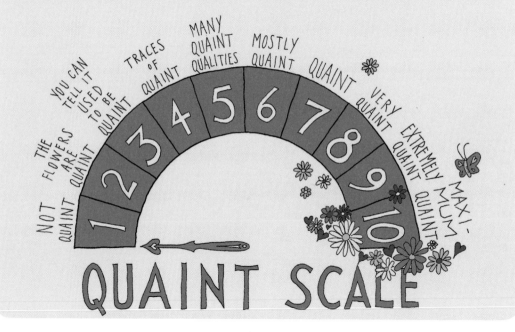

Recommended station cafés and kiosks

1	Inverkeithing (for friendly staff)	6	Sandown
2	Worksop (excellent bacon rolls)	7	Kilmarnock
3	Bridlington (for railway ephemera)	8	Carlisle
4	Irlam	9	King's Lynn (for history)
5	Stalybridge	10	St Erth

CHAPTER

3

DON'T
FORGET
ABOUT THE
NETWORK

DON'T FORGET ABOUT THE NETWORK

When you're travelling around Britain by train, it's likely that where you're going and what you're doing is something you've thought about in advance – you've considered what you're going to see and what you're going to encounter along the way. Your priority is 'Will my train be on time?', particularly if you have multiple connections to make.

But how does your train even get to its destined platform? We learnt a great deal about the complexities of the entire British rail network as we tried to juggle them to stop at every single station in the country.

Depending on how you define them, there are 27 separate train operating companies (TOCs) in Britain, which work together yet are also in competition with each other. (Already it's complicated.) The competition comes from your patronage. Each company wants you to be *their* passenger. There may be more than one company who travels to your intended destination, but who offers the cheapest fare, the quickest service, with the most style or comfort?

But the very fact that companies travel to the same destinations means that they also have to collaborate. They share the same tracks, often the same platforms in stations. In Lancaster, for example, the station is managed and operated by Virgin, but Northern trains also run there and are dispatched by Virgin staff.

And where do Network Rail come into the picture? If the TOCs are running the trains, what do Network Rail do? Well, they actually own all of the network infrastructure: the tracks, the land under the tracks,

Above | Spotted! The Network Rail Operating Centre near Ashburys station in Greater Manchester.

the station buildings, the platforms, the signalling systems and the crossings. They lease stations out to TOCs, who manage and operate services such as ticket offices and the dispatching of trains.

When there are engineering works, or a signal failure, or a 'problem on the line', it's Network Rail who send staff to investigate and manage the problem. They are also the ones who plan ahead, developing upgrade programmes so that the network stays technologically advanced, providing safer, greener and faster services, with the general goal of making the railways a better experience for all. Nothing happens on the network without Network Rail knowing about it.

Then there is the Rail Delivery Group. They work with everyone, all the TOCs, Network Rail, freight operators and everyone in between. They provide information that helps businesses make decisions about changes and improvements to the railway and they also share information to passengers about fares and options for travel. Railcards are a big part of that work, which we inadvertently became something of an expert in as a result of our journey – read on to find out our top tips for money saving as you travel!

We haven't even mentioned the trains themselves (which is a subject of a whole separate chapter) or the companies who manufacture and maintain them for individual TOCs. Train manufacturers have a huge influence on the network – the technologies they adopt or develop affect which systems or infrastructure are advanced or become redundant. Technology which accompanies the new GWR Class 800 trains (soon to be part of Virgin and the new LNER fleets), for example, will come with equipment that digitally scans the trains every time they enter the depot, flagging up potential issues even before they need replacing or fixing. Maintenance will become speedier, and pre-empting problems will mean fewer cancelled trains due to breakdowns or technical faults, more running services, more reliable vehicles, happier customers.

Miraculously – through all this conglomeration of businesses, priorities, data, paperwork, technology and innovation – drivers still manage to turn up at the right station, collect the right train and drive it to where it needs to go. And it's not just drivers, there are guards too. How long are their shifts? What happens if someone is ill or they want to go on holiday? There are the employees who work the catering trolley, and the signallers, the cleaners (or train presentation officers as some of them are known), the platform staff, admin support, schedulers working on the timetables, pest control, British Transport Police, the list goes on and on and on and on.

Of course, it's not always plain sailing (we couldn't think of a train-related pun here, apologies). The disruption caused by timetable changes in May 2018 shows that the systems don't always work. Passengers travelling with train operating companies Northern and Thameslink were most affected when new timetables, rescheduling every single service, were unable to cope with commuter demands. Reports of passengers being stranded for several hours were catastrophic for the reputation of the industry.

But it was our experience that the network is far more complicated and works far better than most people think. After our UK-wide journey in 2017, we calculated that 97.3 per cent of all the trains we travelled on (622 of them) were on time. That is a staggering statistic and a real testament to the jaw-dropping work that everyone does to make it run so smoothly (well, at least 97.3 per cent of the time!).

Next time you catch a train, take a moment to think about all the different facets that make your journey possible. The double arrow symbol you pass on the way in doesn't just denote your station or the TOC you happen to have chosen. It represents the tens of thousands of people who collectively make Britain's railways work. Your train only arrives at its platform because the driver guides it in, because the signaller has given the green light, because the engineer made it safe for operation, because the cleaner tidied up the mess left by passengers the night before, because the guard operated the doors to let passengers on, because the ticket staff sold the tickets to allow passengers to pass through the barriers on the platform where hours earlier the station was closed for engineering works . . .

The intricacies of the network are so rich and so diverse one book cannot possibly cover every single angle. Here's a rundown of some of the most eye-opening and fascinating aspects to look out for as you make your own adventures on the railway.

Above | The CrossCountry service to Manchester Piccadilly from Penzance, in the platform and ready to go.

Train Arranger

Have you ever thought about what happens in a train station at night? No, neither had we. That is until we met Paul, a member of staff at Penzance station. His job, or at least one of the jobs he was doing that evening, was shuffling the trains around to get them in the right starting positions for the next morning.

As soon as Paul explained this, of course it made sense (we think Vicki might have even slapped her hand on her forehead). You can't just put any old random train out there, you need specific trains to travel on specific routes, taking into account platform lengths, estimated passenger numbers, driver capacity, etc. Instructions on what goes where come from somewhere further down the line. Paul showed us a printout that told him in what order to arrange the trains that night. It's something that changes daily, depending on the timetable, whether any trains need to go into the depot for cleaning or repair and if there are any special services running.

It was at this moment that we first realised the huge complexity of the network. The never-ending mass of interwoven operations that go into making everything run as smoothly as possible. Stuff that goes on that the public rarely get to see or, like us, even know is taking place.

'Shuffling trains around like a giant game of Tetris'

While we're all tucked up in bed, people like Paul, in stations all over the country, are shuffling trains around like a giant game of Tetris, getting ready for it to all start again in the morning.

Vicki: I like to think there is some kind of train shuffling league. Where staff across the country log the number of trains they've shuffled each week, how many moves it took them and the equivalent distance they travelled while shuffling. Prizes for those who did it in the most efficient way possible.

'All trains on the network have their path to follow'

The Scheduler

Ah yes, *schedules*. As you can imagine, the biggest challenge of trying to stop at all 2,563 stations in Britain was understanding the scheduling patterns of EVERY service on the network. Needless to say, we had help. Mainly from our trusted scheduler extraordinaire Mr Dave Green, but also from others along the way. If you live or work in and around cities like Manchester, Birmingham, Cardiff, Glasgow or London you'll be familiar with services that run at a certain minute past or to the hour, maybe as frequently as every 15 minutes. The further away from these more densely populated places you get, typically the longer the time between services becomes, an hour or two hours in some places, up to four hours is not uncommon or – as we've also seen – several days in between.

Then there are fast and stopping trains, what is known as the *skip-stop* pattern of services. In its simplest form, if you have a line with ten stations from A to J then the train company send the fast train first, departing station A, perhaps stopping at station E only, before terminating at station J. Back at station A the slow-stopping train then calls at every station on the line. If it was done the other way around, the fast train would be held up by the stopper.

That's not the only way of doing it though, as we discovered on the line from Liverpool Street through Colchester to the seaside destinations of either Clacton-on-Sea or Walton-on-the-Naze. Here they *do* do it the other way around, in a clever way. The stopping train heading for Walton-on-the-Naze 'goes' first and plods off along the line, then at its allotted time the fast train starts behind it. The fast train bound for Clacton then catches up with it at the junction that is Thorpe-le-

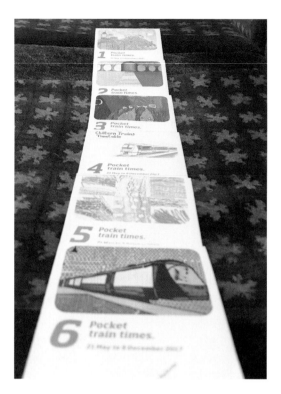

Soken station. If you are on the fast train and want to go to Walton-on-the-Naze, you can cross over to the slow train here. It's an interesting way of doing it, but one that relies on some smart scheduling and the trains remaining absolutely on time.

We take the concept and idea of a train timetable so much for granted now, but who devised the original schedule when the first passenger trains began operating? In London, when the Metropolitan Railway opened in 1863 (what became the Met line on the Tube), trains ran every 20 minutes off peak, and every 15 minutes at other times. From the very beginning there was someone in charge of scheduling the correct number of trains for every service and destination.

Of all the schedules across the country, there is one that still to this day we cannot fathom out. That is the Chiltern Railways stopping pattern, masterminded, we truly believe, by an

Above | The Chiltern Railways stopping pattern may be difficult to fathom, but their timetable covers are lovely and those pictured were all created by school children from along the Chiltern network.

evil genius. Download it for yourself and have a go. It makes *Finnegans Wake* look like a Thomas the Tank Engine storybook. It seems to defy logic, we can't find a pattern in it, just a random collection of times. We'd really like to meet the person who devises Chiltern's timetables. Do get in touch if you're reading this!

To be fair, we can see *some* reasoning behind it. The trains coming in and out of Marylebone through the Chilterns and up to Birmingham do so on just two tracks. There's no additional third or fourth tracks here to allow for 'fast' and 'stopping' services to be separated, and it's just not possible to stop all services at all the stations. However, the pattern that's used – well, it's not a pattern. See comments above.

It took until we got to Swindon for us to encounter anyone with any real responsibility for timetabling. An aside about Swindon – it is steeped in railway history. Just a short walk from the station is the STEAM museum (which tells the story of the Great Western Railway) and the old Swindon Railway Works (repair sheds for GWR steam engines, now a shopping and business centre) and a railway village (with preserved railway worker cottages). GWR still have a lot of

Above | Today the modern exterior of Swindon station gives little to no clue of the deep-rooted connection the area has with the railways.

offices here for their current workforce, and it was one of them who we bumped into on the train from Swindon to Westbury. Seb, the Saturday Timetable Manager.

'*Saturday* scheduler?' asked Geoff. 'Surely you're just one big scheduling team?' Not so, explained Seb. As it turns out there are different teams of people, for the weekday timetable, the Saturday timetable, and then, for the quietest of all days, a team that works on the Sunday timetable.

Our biggest question for Seb was, in reality, how much do timetables change? (Perhaps a silly question in light of the recent changes). The answer is that they evolve. Typically, you always need your morning and evening peak services, people flocking in their thousands

towards conurbations and back out again. But the part in between, daytime and weekend travelling, is up for grabs. To help devise the right schedule you need to take into account trends in shopping and holiday travel, the seasons, local and national events. But to what extent are these trends natural or are they in fact dictated by the railways themselves? Take Sundays for example, is it really just the quietest day on the network or is it *because* train companies typically run fewer services on those days that it is quiet?

We spoke to Seb at length about the service we were then on, the Swindon to Westbury that stopped at Melksham en route. As recently as 2013, Melksham only had two trains a day that stopped (one on Sunday), but with a timetable change it now sees services stopping every two hours. 'It's not just a simple case of saying a train can stop more,' explained Seb. 'You have to look at the knock-on effects it has to other routes.' And this includes freight routes too.

All trains on the network have their 'paths' to follow. A path is the calculated amount of time and space taken by each train that passes through a given section of the railway. Ultimately there is only a finite number of trains you can put through every section of track during a set period of time. You can't just arbitrarily send as many trains as you like along a route, mostly because of the constraints of the signalling system, which requires every train to be a specified distance over a signal before it is deemed clear and safe for the next train to proceed.

It is the job of schedulers like Seb to work all this out. To juggle the trains and decide the stopping patterns to meet the needs of the public, to adhere to the amount of spare paths available and to put together a timetable.

Geoff: An indicator of how timetables have changed can be seen in railway crossings. Take Lincoln, for example. There is a crossing just outside the station along the high street, the busiest road in the city, and the barrier goes up and down every few minutes. It delays road traffic and people, although a new passenger footbridge has been built to help people cross while the barriers are down. If you were building a station today it would be very silly to put a crossing in the middle of the high street. It's an indication of how few trains passed through then compared to now.

Single Tracks and their Tokens

Vicki: On the very first day of our adventure Geoff got chatting to a driver at St Erth station. Geoff beckoned me over and the driver handed me a wooden staff. 'That's for staff working,' he said. I had no idea what he was talking about.

The driver further explained. Where there is a branch line with only a single track connecting each station, the driver with the right of way is denoted by the possession of a token. At St Erth this token is a wooden staff, in other places it's a metal ring or disc.

It was like we'd stepped back in time. We couldn't believe that in an age of driverless trains, a humble wooden staff token still existed.

Tokens are collected by the driver just before the start of a single-track section, which could be anywhere along a given route. The driver might collect and return the token from a secured box on the platform of the closest station or be handed it by a signaller from a nearby lineside box or junction. If the train you're on slows down somewhere other than a station, it could be the driver collecting the token.

At St Erth it seemed particularly bizarre. The line down to St Ives is all single track and takes 28 minutes to traverse. Even though just one solitary train unit goes back and forth all day and so, er, has no chance of crashing into . . . itself . . . the driver still requires the token in order to pull the train out of the station. This is the simplest form of single track and is known as 'one train working'. Incidentally, the token at St Erth is thought to be the original, nearly 150 years old. Mind. Blown.

'Mind. Blown.'

Once you've noticed one single-track line, you can't help but keep noticing them, and you wonder why you've never noticed them before. You might think that it's perhaps just small local lines (like the St Ives branch) that are single track, but it's not. There are major railway lines with long, large trains carrying hundreds of commuters that are all single track too.

The most obvious example is the Cotswolds Line, which passes through little-used Combe station in Oxfordshire. This is a major route from Oxford through to Worcester and Hereford and it *used* to be all double track. (Geeky fact for you: it was almost built to Brunel's

Above | Platform 3 at St Erth station. The dedicated platform for the 'one train working' to St Ives.

wider gauge of seven-and-a-quarter feet, but costs meant that it was built to standard gauge instead.) If you get out at any of the stations, Finstock is a great example, you can clearly see where the other track and platforms used to be. Or look out for road bridges by the stations along the line that are wide enough for two tracks but there's only one running underneath. If the track was doubled between Worcester and Hereford, that would allow both London–Hereford and Birmingham–Hereford services to be hourly. Just saying.

By the time this book is published, Britain's 2,564th railway station will have opened at Kenilworth, and the line there, between Leamington and Coventry, is also single track. In the south-east of England the Hurst Green to Uckfield line has single track sections; Ormskirk to Preston in the north, and between Perth to Inverness in Scotland are also single track.

The argument is that having a single track saves money, because double tracks obviously double maintenance costs. But what is more cost efficient? Having a single track and enduring delays, or having the higher cost and offsetting that against not having hold-ups both ways on the line? Discuss among yourself and get back to us, thanks.

'Like an AA or RAC roadside assistant'

Above | Inside Ilford Depot where engineers work night and day to keep trains on track to provide a good service.

The Roving Engineer

When you think of train maintenance (as we know you often do) you will likely think about a large depot, full of trains, with engineers in hi-vis safety attire underneath or inside vehicles, covered in dirt, tightening something with a spanner or rewiring a circuit somewhere.

You're not wrong necessarily, and this certainly is the case for a large majority of maintenance facilities throughout the country (though technology now plays such a large part some engineers' jobs can be significantly computer based). Indeed, we saw this first-hand at the train care maintenance depot in Ilford, where we had been invited by Dan, who worked for Greater Anglia.

In the depot there were wheel lathes, gigantic cranes for lifting heavy gear, the bogey pit (no sniggering please), shelves upon shelves of boxes containing tools, train parts, nuts and bolts, moquette that was too soiled to be in service, spare network maps (the kind you

Above | Can you tell we were excited to look round Ilford Depot?!

see inside trains that show you the route you're travelling along), in fact anything and everything you might possibly need to fix, clean and revamp a train. The volume of work is constant, there are approximately 300 staff that work in the Ilford Depot alone, with teams of engineers working 24 hours a day to keep on top of all the jobs. Sometimes a fault gets reported in the morning, it arrives in the depot during the day and by evening rush hour it's out again on the network, such is the sleight of hand of the engineer!

Dan's job wasn't just confined to the depot, however. He was what we later coined a 'roving engineer'. Again, a job we had no idea existed or had even contemplated would exist, but now seems like a crucial role. When trains break down on the network Dan can be called to fix things on-site. Imagine him like an AA or RAC roadside assistant, except trackside for getting broken-down trains on the go instead.

'I never know where I'm going to be one day to the next, which is one of the best parts, but also really tiring,' Dan told us. When he books on for work, he could have a quiet day pootling around the depot or he could be dispatched at a moment's notice up to Ipswich, out to Clacton or to a 'local' job, say in Colchester. He could be a few minutes or he could be several hours out in the field, trying to get a train back up and running.

Dan was so enthusiastic, it was clear he really loved his job, even though sometimes it can be more than just technically challenging. An eye-opening moment for us was when Dan talked briefly about being required to attend an incident when someone has been hit by a train. An engineer is called so they can advise the emergency services about which parts of the train can be moved or removed, or the best way to access certain sections of the vehicle. Sometimes this involves getting up close to the person who has died, or is trapped. Dan spoke about it like it was just another aspect of his work, but it made us realise that it's not just the emergency services who work hard to care for passengers after an incident.

'It's one of
the most
challenging
roles on the
entire network'

The Guard

If we were to be completely honest with you, if you asked us the difference between a guard, a conductor and a train manager we're not sure we could tell you. Essentially, they all do the same job, but we suspect that different train operating companies like to give their staff different titles, so it varies from place to place. To try to keep things nice and simple we're going to go with the traditional title of 'the guard' for this section of the book, just so we're clear.

One of the greatest debates going on right now is: should all trains have guards? Our view is: yes. Not only are guards an endless source of useful and insightful information, and chatting to them is a great way to spend some of your journey, having a guard on the train adds an additional sense of security, and if there is an emergency it's better to have two members of staff to deal with the situation that just one. We also wonder what might happen if the driver in a driver-only train themselves becomes incapacitated, what would happen then? For these reasons and more, we're in favour of guards.

Having travelled on 622 trains during our adventure we met a significant number of guards and noticed that everyone had their own inimitable style and way of doing things. Some are very protective, they feel it's 'their train' and not the driver's; they're the one who clears the doors and tells the driver when it's safe for them to leave, so therefore they are in charge. Some are an absolute hoot! The gentleman on our Sheringham train gave very lyrical announcements and made everyone on the train smile as he walked by making jokes and chatting away as he collected tickets. The guard on one of the Southern services was so surprised we wanted to chat it took three attempts for him to realise we weren't trying to make a complaint (poor Southern, they really were having a bad time of it in 2017). Almost without exception (OK, yes, there *were* two exceptions, but we don't want to give them credit in the book) guards were friendly, approachable and happy to chat, and were the best source of information we could find.

But what do they actually do? Again this varies from one train operating company to another, but for the majority their role encompasses operational aspects of the train journey: checking and selling tickets, making announcements about the arrival times at stations and any issues or delays that might affect passengers along the way, letting

Above | Phil our guard at Wigan on Northern Railway. Phil is also a fellow Pacer fan, good man! (Find out more about our love of Pacers in chapter 5.)

people on and off by operating the doors (particularly important if stations have a short platform), informing the driver of any request stops as well as helping with faults or problems along the track. We saw a guard once having to alight from the train ahead of a station to manage road traffic at a crossing where the barriers had failed to go down. There is also the people side of the role – dispensing information, managing angry or upset passengers, issuing fines for those without valid tickets or at least a valid reason for not having a ticket, and dealing with emergencies if passengers are unwell or become violent. There are so many facets to being a guard, so many versatile skills you need to do it well, that we feel it's one of the most challenging roles on the entire network.

Because of the range of skills required, people come to the job from lots of different backgrounds. We met guards who were former train drivers, lorry drivers, police officers, soldiers and even bank managers. Lots of guards have family connections to the railways – their parents used to work on the railways, or their partners do and they lured them in. Some guards are what is known as 'lifers', which means that they've worked on the railways their entire adult life and plan on doing so until they retire. Everyone had an interesting story to tell, which is another great reason to get to know your guard.

And because guards tend to work a series of particular routes, if you are a regular traveller you will likely see the same faces regularly, so why not say hello? One of our favourite guards we met was Paul in Wales, on Cardiff's Valley Lines. Of the five trains we caught one day, we saw Paul three times! 'Oh, it's you guys again,' he said, cheerfully grinning, and waved his hand at us already knowing that we had valid tickets. If only we had guards on our local services, we thought, it would be like seeing an old friend at the start or end of your day!

Paul was lovely and took time to chat to us, and give us local insight and history into the Valleys, its history with the mining industry and how the railways are essential to get people to where the majority of the jobs are in Cardiff. We really wanted to go down the pub and talk more with him, but we had stations to visit and he had a train to safely dispatch.

Accessibility

One of the greatest areas in need of improvement across the network is accessibility for passengers who require additional support when travelling. This includes better step-free access into stations and onto trains, information and signage in multiple formats (for example, larger font or braille), hearing loops or audiovisual guides both in stations and on vehicles, as well as training for staff to understand and offer help for passengers.

'Support shouldn't be tokenistic, it should be appropriate and meaningful'

There is often no consistency across the network even at stations. The format of signage in one area of the country is sometimes different in another. You are reliant on members of staff who, through no fault of their own, can be delayed or given misinformation. We spoke to passengers who told us that as wheelchair users they have sometimes been left for anywhere between ten and thirty minutes waiting for a member of staff to bring a ramp to help them alight the train. By which time they'd missed their connection or the appointment that they were heading to.

We understand that the circumstances are challenging. Some parts of the network are over 150 years old, and the majority of trains and buildings were designed and built long before considerations about accessibility. There is a lot to do. And there *are* some great changes being made. The British government has an active plan to address many of these issues in compliance with the EU's regulation on 'technical specifications for interoperability relating to accessibility of the Unions rail systems for persons with disabilities and persons with reduced mobility' (PRM-TSI for short). This includes a programme of large-scale funding for station upgrade work – allocated against criteria of industry priorities, passenger footfall, number of people registered as disabled or accessing services for their disability in the local area, geographic location and opportunities for additional funding. Smaller pots of money are also available to individual TOCs, though when awarded it is up to them how they spend it.

The downside is that funding is only available until 2019, after which a new strategy will, we assume, be implemented. The plan for vehicle upgrades is slightly different, with funding committed to achieving a target of 100 per cent compliance by 2020 (bye-bye Pacer trains!).

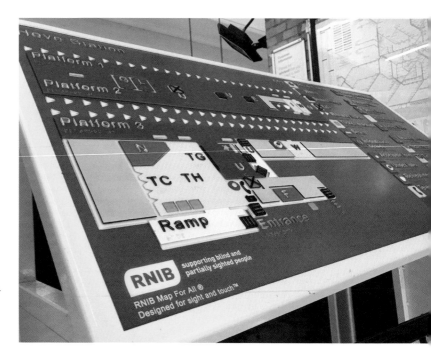

Right | The RNIB Map For All is available in some, but not all, stations around the country. The map uses a mix of visual and tactile elements to enable anyone to access it no matter what their needs.

One of the greatest opportunities for better access is when new stations are built. Cambridge North station opened as we were travelling around the country, on 21 May 2017. We made a visit just two weeks later, excited to see such a shiny new station and to understand what made this so distinct from other stations in this area. There were lots of great details, and we were particularly interested to see Braille on the stairs' handrails. We thought this small intervention must make a difference to lots of travellers, helping to give them more confidence to use the station independently. It wasn't until later, when we posted our video online, that some of our followers told us that actually the Braille had been put on backwards.

Below | Braille information on the handrails at Cambridge North station as installed in 2017.

This did make us wonder about the process of developing new accessible features at stations. Who is consulted? In the case of Cambridge North, did someone actually check with a Braille reader which way round to install the signs or was it a simple mistake? There can be guidelines and laws in place about the incorporation of certain accessible requirements, but unless you actually need to use step-free access or a hearing loop, for example, how can you understand the best way to implement them? Sadly we didn't meet anyone working in this area of the network to find out more about the changes taking place. But from conversations with passengers and followers, it's clear that support of any kind shouldn't be tokenistic, it should be appropriate and meaningful to those you hope will benefit from it. And the only way to find out if it will is to ask.

Ticketing

We feel strongly that we can't write a book about railways, and particularly one which encourages you – the reader – to go out and have your own adventure, without talking about tickets. If you're going to take a train, you're going to need to buy a ticket. Them's the rules.

Having chatted to ticket staff and passengers about their tickets we have accumulated a broad knowledge, which – to paraphrase Baz Luhrmann – we would like, to dispense, to you now.

Mobile Tickets

Today, there may be 27 different train operating companies that offer various ticket prices and options, but at least there are websites and ticket machines at stations where you can just type in where you want to go, and it (hopefully) works out the best price for you. (There are also ticket staff in some stations who you can actually talk to. Retro.)

Go back in time to when the railways first started in the 1800s. Every train company who built a line was completely independent of each other. Their only concern was to make money for themselves and that meant you had buy a separate ticket for all of them. Great examples are Catford and Catford Bridge, which are 20 seconds' walk apart. (Literally. You could actually throw a stone from one to the other.) Built separately by different train companies, they too would have had different ticket-issuing systems.

More strange examples of non-joined-up ticketing systems can be found on the London Underground. What we know today as the Northern Line started out life as the 'Hampstead Tube' down one branch, and the City & South London Railway along the other. When the two lines met and 'linked up' at Euston in the 1920s, an interchange corridor was built underground to change between the two. But you still had to buy a separate ticket, which is why (uniquely) the remains of a subterranean ticket office still exist today.

In London now, the entire system is joined up following the introduction of the Oyster card in 2003, and more recently you can just use your contactless debit or credit card. And main line TOCs are starting to get in on the action with their own non-ticket solutions. Southeastern run a system called The Key, where you just load your ticket (usually a season ticket) onto a card and you tap in (like Oyster) at the station to make your journey. No physical tickets required any more.

Then there is a whole new dimension of ticketing – mobile tickets, or m-Tickets as they are also known. These are purchased on your smartphone, via one of the official rail apps, and are then download to your device. Voila! The ticket is on your phone, you can show it to the guard and use it at a barrier, that's it. Is it the future? Quite possibly, yes.

But the future is not quite everywhere just yet. Not all ticket barriers at stations have the appropriate scanners. In which case, you can still purchase your ticket on your phone, via your chosen app, but instead of a barcode, you get a confirmation code and you then have to pick up your tickets from a machine at the station. Just the same as if you were buying online through a regular web browser.

One of the biggest questions people raise about mobile tickets is the validity. Surely you could just keep using the same ticket over and over again? Each app works slightly differently, but no, you need to 'activate' the ticket when you're ready to use it, so that if it's inspected by a guard they know it's a 'live' ticket, and not just a screenshot of one that you may have bought previously. There's still some element of the human touch needed.

We tried out mobile ticketing for one day in the Sheffield and Leeds area, and we did wonder what would happen when the guards came to inspect us, but there were no issues at all. 'Oh, we've all been trained on these,' our guard told us cheerfully. 'There were a few teething problems when they first came in, but now they're becoming quite a regular thing.'

Breaking Your Journey

If you purchase a 'flexible ticket' (usually *not* an advance ticket where you have to be on a specific train) you may not know that you are allowed to 'break your journey' en route.

It sounds all rather painful, but trust us, nothing could be more simple. And it could give you a great opportunity to have a quick explore of an area or station you've never been to before. It works best if you have, say, 20 minutes at a station where you are making a connection to a different service. You're perfectly entitled to go through the ticket barrier, dash to the shops or look outside (take a picture of the station if it's a nice one) and then come back in again to catch your next train and continue your journey. Even better, if you're not in a rush, you could arrange to meet a friend for a cuppa somewhere nearby. Put your physical ticket into the ticket gate (or scan your mobile ticket) and collect it again, and it will let you through the gateline, and then let you back in again when you want to carry on with your journey.

Just remember, you're allowed to break your journey at any station along the way if your ticket says 'Any Permitted' on it, but you *can't* do this if your ticket says 'Booked Train Only'. These are special low-price tickets, and the reason they're low price is because you really do have to be on the specific train that you booked and thus no breaking the journey for you. Sorry.

Cheaper Ticket Tricks

Considering that people often comment on the price of tickets in Britain – and it's true, the latest figures show that a commuter may spend up to 13 per cent of their salary on an annual season ticket to get to work, while in other places in Europe it's usually somewhere between 2 and 5 per cent – we're sure you'll want to know ways you can make a journey for less.

Advance tickets

To start with, if you can, always book your journey in advance. We know this doesn't work for everyone but sometimes you can see strange special offers if you book early enough. We once saw Virgin Trains offer First Class tickets *cheaper* than the Standard Class fares. We did it just for the free tea! The earlier you book, the cheaper it is, and you can book up to 12 weeks in advance, too.

If you do this, you'll get what's known as an Advance ticket. You can buy these right up to midnight the day before travel, but the closer to the day, the more expensive they become. So do book ahead if you can.

In some cases, you find ridiculously cheap tickets that stipulate that you must travel on the specified train. This comes up as 'Booked Train Only' on your ticket. There are some real bargains to be had, but the downside is that they're not flexible and you *must* travel on the train specified on your ticket or you'll be liable to pay the full fare – and get a stern telling off from the guard.

Permit To Travel

Time

15:50

When lit   When lit

Not in use

00.00

Amount paid

5p 10p 20p 50p £1

No change given

≋ Permit To Travel

This machine will issue a Permit To Travel unless otherwise indicated by the red light(s).

To obtain a Permit To Travel

1. Insert coins to the value of the fare due for your journey. If you have insufficient coins to pay the full fare please insert the maximum possible towards the fare and a Permit To Travel may be obtained for part payment. Amount paid will be displayed.

2. Press the green button to obtain your Permit To Travel upon which the amount paid will be printed.

For conditions of issue and use of Permits To Travel please see separate notice.

1. Insert coins

2. Press for Permit

Rejected coins

Split ticketing

Many people consider split ticketing to be some kind of dark art, but really it's just being extremely savvy about where you get your tickets from. It's a more lengthy process to go through when purchasing, but it can save you oodles of money. Here's how to do it.

If you are travelling from station A to F, and your train also stops at B, C, D and E along the way, it *may* be cheaper to buy a ticket from A–D and then D–F, rather than get the standard price for the full A–F ticket. We know it sounds crazy, but it is true. You can either experiment online yourself, or use websites which specialise in split ticketing, they will tell you where to make the 'splits', giving you an overall cheaper journey. Huzzah!

Railcards

Railcards are a great way to save money, but unfortunately not everyone can get one. There are eight main railcards in Britain (16–25, 26–30, Senior, Disabled, Two-Together, Family, Network and Gold Card) and generally speaking they give you 1/3 discount on off-peak travel. Almost all ticket offices at all stations in the country have leaflets in the ticket racks with details on them, and you can buy them at any ticket office. They all have slightly different restrictions and terms of use, but overall if you are a regular traveller they will save you money.

And then, for ultimate ticketing kudos, if you combine Advance tickets with a railcard, you can often get some absolute bargains. At the time of writing, we just bought First Class tickets from London to Norwich for only £9 each, which is a freaking steal.

Rover tickets

Rover tickets (or Rail Rovers) are special tickets that cover a specific *area* rather than an A–B journey. Rovers are usually valid for just one day, though there are exceptions. The Devon Day Ranger, for example, costs just £12 and lets you travel anywhere along the Gunnislake branch, Paignton branch, Barnstaple branch, Exmouth branch and as far east as Tiverton Parkway and Axminster. If you're making multiple trips, it easily beats the costs of buying multiple tickets – it's a no-brainer to get one.

All Rover ticket options are listed on the National Rail website and this leads us to possibly our greatest money-saving tip of all: why not split your journey and make one of your tickets a Rover? i.e. It's sometimes possible to buy a ticket to the edge of an area that a Rover covers, then buy a Rover for the rest of the journey, and the cost of those two combined are cheaper than if you a buy a ticket all the way through. We did this recently on a day out from London to Exeter and saved ourselves £30!

GroupSave

An amazing way to save money which very few people know about. If there is a group of you travelling (three to nine people) then you can buy what's known as a GroupSave ticket and immediately get one third off the total price. Simple as that. It's a bit like having a Three-Together railcard, except you don't need a railcard, you just need three or more people!

There is admittedly a caveat to this though – *not* all the TOCs do it. It seems to be the ones in the south-east of England, but also West Midland Trains, GWR and ScotRail. If you're buying your ticket online, websites often don't offer this up for you automatically – instead, choose 'Railcard' then select 'GroupSave' to get the money off. We often tell people who have *never* heard of this before, and later they come back to us slightly overjoyed. 'We saved a third off!' they tell us. 'We know!' we reply, smiling.

Days Out Guide

Finally, the other great thing about your train ticket is that it doesn't just allow you to journey along the network, it can also help you get two-for-one entry at tourist destinations around the country (it's like businesses don't want to make money).

The offer, provided by Days Out Guide (in partnership with National Rail) is only valid on specific types of train tickets and at certain venues, so make sure you have a good read on their website of all the T&Cs before you commit to making the journey. Here at All The Stations HQ, we have used the offer a few times to get into some of the more expensive attractions and it made a big difference to our tea and cake kitty for the day.

And here endeth our sermon on how to enjoy cheaper fares the next time you're buying tickets. And if you've got this far in the book and you're not itching to go on a railway journey yet, then *what the heck is wrong with you?!* You really should already be planning your next railway adventure . . .

The most impressive stations in Great Britain

As we travelled across the network we were surprised and delighted by so many stations, but there were lots that had that extra special something – they left an indelible impression on our memories. After much deliberation we created our list of Britain's Top Ten Most Impressive Stations and then soon wondered what other people might consider impressive or memorable themselves. So, we put it to a public vote. The results are in ...

Vicki and Geoff's list

1 Wemyss Bay
2 Birmingham Moor Street
3 Manchester Victoria
4 York
5 Bristol Temple Meads (pictured here)
6 Ramsgate
7 Preston
8 Glasgow Central
9 Huddersfield
10 Shrewsbury

The public vote

1 Huddersfield
2 London St Pancras International
3 Wemyss Bay
4 York
5 Bristol Temple Meads
6 London Paddington
7 Glasgow Central
8 London King's Cross
9 Birmingham Moor Street
10 Corrour

4

CHAPTER

TALK TO AS MANY PEOPLE AS YOU CAN

TALK TO AS MANY PEOPLE AS YOU CAN

People are brilliant. There, we said it and we regret nothing. The news will, nine times out of ten, run stories that focus on the bad side of human nature. Every magazine on the newsagent's shelves is packed with negative images of celebrities, break-ups, betrayal, law suits. The internet can often be a megaphone for people to express how annoyed by stuff or other people they are. Perhaps that's why everyone goes crazy for kitten GIFs and inspirational quotes Photoshopped onto the background of whimsical landscapes – we're all eager to see and do something good. OK, we accept that not ALL people are universally great, but after more than 15 weeks travelling the length and breadth of the country we discovered only a handful of people who were reluctant to chat (and we're willing to concede that perhaps even they were likely just having a bad day, or had missed their morning caffeine hit).

From the very beginning, people were at the heart of our adventure. We didn't just go to those places that *we* thought were interesting. We'd never even been to Bridlington for goodness' sake, what did we know! Who better to tell you what a place is really like then those who live there themselves? We asked the internet, 'Tell us the places you think we should go to and why?' and the internet responded, with thousands of messages. So much so it was very hard to keep up. A monsoon of tweets, Facebook messages, Instagram messages (we

'People are brilliant'

Above | Crabbing is a popular pastime it seems in Lowestoft, and the secret to this family's success? Bacon.

didn't even know that was a thing!), emails, hand-written portfolios (we're not even joking), accostings in the street and letters poured in. There were endless stories to draw on, endless things to see, endless contacts in endless places offering help – guided tours, a lift, a supply of tea. 'If you come to my town, please let me know and I can show you round.'

One of the strongest messages that came through was how passionate people are about their home town. Early on, we received a wonderful message from Mark, who lives in Suffolk. He offered himself up as a guide to the railways and local history in and around Lowestoft (local dialect guide: forget the 'e' and go straight into the 'stoft'). When eventually we arrived, Mark didn't just tell us a few anecdotes or point out a few local plaques, he had reference material and gave up half of his day to show us around. Nothing was too much trouble, even when we got a bit distracted capturing some drone footage and ended up chatting to a local family, who then showed us how to go crabbing. Mark joined in, answered all our questions and gave us an insight into the area which we could never have gained by ourselves alone.

Did you know, Lowestoft was famous for red herring? That's not a red herring, it actually was. The town was shaped by the industry and the railway played a part, as the line extended into the harbour to enable

Above | North Denes. These wooden beams symbolise the town's once thriving fishing industry.

produce to be easily transported inland. One of the most fascinating landmarks is what at first glance looks like a random assortment of wooden beams in the middle of a patch of wasteland (sorry North Denes). In fact, they hold a lot of significance to the town's social history. It is where fishing nets would have been hung to dry and be repaired, vital to the livelihood of local fishermen and a job mostly carried out by women.

Never underestimate local knowledge; there is only so much the internet can tell you.

The level of generosity from people was something neither of us had experienced before. It fuelled our determination to keep going (particularly during those moments when we felt most tired and unclear why we'd started this outrageous adventure in the first place) and it genuinely changed our perspective – not just our knowledge – about different parts of the country. We'd always thought of Manchester, for example, as quite a nostalgic, hard-edged, heavily industrialised city with lots of grit and grime. But when we met with Karl and he told us more about his experience of the changing landscape of the city, particularly the development of local transport infrastructure – the success of the tram network and plans for new and better-connected services between Manchester Piccadilly and Victoria stations – we saw the city in a new light. Far from being stuck in the past, Manchester is a bright, modern city in a constant cycle of regeneration, always growing and improving on the previous idea. There is a wonderful blending of the past with areas of cultural significance (such as Chetham's Library – one of the oldest public libraries in the world!) and modern feats of architectural prowess. We now understand why the bee is such a good symbol for the city, it really is a hive of activity – always striving to create something new.

On your own adventures, as well as arranging to meet specific people (not necessarily random strangers from the internet like us, but friends, family or an old colleague you've not seen for a few years),

Above | Weymouth Harbour may look beautiful now, but in the fourteenth century this was the gateway for the Black Death . . .

don't forget your fellow passengers. Sometimes a trip on a train is just that, a journey from A to B. Nothing happens in between – maybe you read a book, maybe you listen to some music, maybe you watch a movie, some of you might even do some knitting (we found Emerson Park is a great station to indulge in a bit of knitting, just FYI), then you arrive at your destination. It's a functional process, and that's all there is to it. But it doesn't have to be.

Of course, the decision to talk should always be mutual. If you ever feel uncomfortable or pressurised, or in a dangerous situation, you should report it to a member of staff. But you can have a far more enjoyable experience if you talk to people along the way. Most are very pleased to chat, like the two ladies we struck up a conversation with on the train from Westbury to Weymouth. They told us about the local area, the best things to do and see during the evening (which for the record is to get fish and chips in Weymouth Harbour – delicious!), and then somehow got embroiled in a very good-natured but none-the-less passionate debate about whether Weymouth town or the Isle of Portland was the better place to live. It turns out there is little to choose between the two, except that it was through the port of Weymouth that the Black Death came to the Britain in the fourteenth century. We're not saying the people of the Isle of Portland are the kind to hold a grudge, but . . .

This type of joyful conversation was a regular occurrence. Even on our very last trip from Inverness to Wick, we chatted to a couple sitting just across the aisle from us and discovered they'd had their wedding ceremony on a train, because in Scotland the law is different and you can get married anywhere. Literally anywhere. We had no idea!

By talking to people and asking questions we didn't just travel to every station, we gained an insight into the importance of these stations and the services the railways provide. Some people talked about the independence the railways give them, for others it is a way to maintain friendships or a relationship with family members they would otherwise not be able to see. For many it provides a crucial link to medical treatment, opportunities for work or education or even just a chance to explore and learn about communities outside of their own.

It would be impossible to include the stories of everyone we met, but we wanted to share some of the encounters that stuck with us and helped us to better understand the way the network impacts people and their communities.

Oh, and don't forget. People are brilliant, talk to as many of them as you can.

Below | Geoff and Mark walking along Ness Point in Lowestoft (England's most easterly point). The wind turbine is known locally as Gulliver and is approximately 126 metres (413 feet) tall.

Local Guides

Daryl of Haverfordwest/Hwlffordd

Local businessman, radio DJ (tune into Pure West Radio on Wednesday and Friday nights), occasional bar keep, photo journalist and general all-round nice guy, Daryl contacted us via Facebook before we'd even set out on our journey. He offered us fascinating insights into the town of Haverfordwest, knowledge about the railways of South Wales (including a familial connection through his grandfather 'Dusty', who was employed as a fireman during the grand age of steam) and recommendations of where to stay.

When we arrived at the town's only station, Daryl was there to meet us and (once we'd appeased the advances of two local journalists) we quickly got chatting. Daryl was easy to talk to and very relaxing to be around. We felt very welcomed and were soon privy to lots of local knowledge. Like many people we had met, Daryl talked with passion and affection about his home town, but also with realism about the difficulties the town faces; particularly the struggle to compete for trade and tourism with other South Wales towns. Though he wasn't without hope for the future.

'Ah, you must be from up the line'

Above | The weir and salmon ladder on the Western Cleddau.

One of the most interesting things we learnt from Daryl was Pembrokeshire's use of the Welsh language. Intriguingly it seems that in this part of the country the railways emphasise a language barrier between those who speak Welsh and those who don't. This divide was once so strong that the area south-west of the tracks was known as 'Little England Beyond Wales' – some people still refer to it as such – where only English was spoken. Conversely on the opposite side people predominantly spoke Welsh. This border, also known as the Landsker Line, was not defined geographically by the railway but was more a colloquial term of reference. In fact, the phrase 'up the line' is still used in the context of identifying those with a stronger Welsh accent: 'Ah, you must be from up the line.'

Haverfordwest/Hwlffordd, though the county town of Pembrokeshire, is in fact middling in size and small enough that as we walked around several people stopped us to say hello to Daryl in passing. Or perhaps this is simply a result of Daryl being active in different aspects of town life; he has experienced the community from lots of different perspectives and as such we could not have had a better guide.

Historically the town has been a prime location for invasion and settlement – by the Romans, the Flemish and the English, to name a few. It flourished as a market town, being along the main trade routes in the

area and with a once-bustling port on the Western Cleddau River, with goods arriving regularly from Bristol. The main traffic up the river now is fish, particularly salmon who have their own ladder with webcam so you can watch them make their way upstream.

The town centre today is made up of an eclectic mix of modern shops and historic buildings. There is a castle (hurrah!), which Oliver Cromwell ordered to be destroyed in the seventeenth century. Needless to say its destruction did not take place, despite threats from Cromwell to put all the town's inhabitants under garrison. You can read these threats in a series of letters he wrote to the town, now on display in the local museum – ironically housed within the castle grounds.

Currently the rail service to this part of Wales is minimal. During the day, a train runs approximately every two hours in either direction. If you fancy a night out in Cardiff the last service back leaves Cardiff Queen Street at around 9 p.m. The positive side to so few trains, says Daryl, is that there's less chance of being delayed. But the importance of the railways is acute to everyone, particularly those, like Daryl, who run a business. The railways provide visitors and if there were more regular services this would dramatically improve the economy of the local area, giving the town the much-needed boost it deserves.

Ceci in Oxford

Oxford. A place everyone has heard of. Packed with history, tradition, intellectuals, bikes, punts and multiple *Harry Potter* locations.

Vicki: If I'd have had my way I would have tried to at least engineer one or two days in Oxford. But the timetables were against me and Geoff was against me, and so it was that we had just an hour. ONE HOUR. To try to encapsulate all that is Oxford. This, I thought, is not possible. Enter Ceci.

'Tour guide extraordinaire'

Ceci wasn't just prepared, she had performed reconnaissance trips to time the quickest routes from the station into the key sightseeing locations of the city. She had even cleared it with staff at Divinity Hall that we could film inside the building (something regular visitors are not normally allowed to do). No detail was left to chance. Not even the possibility that we might miss each other at the station, for Ceci had created a sign to hold up, like taxi drivers do when meeting

people off flights at the airport, so we could spot her as we exited the ticket barriers.

Our tour didn't just focus on the things you can see and should probably come back and visit properly later; Ceci really gave us a flavour of what it's like to live and work in Oxford today. Unlike some other historical cities where modern life exists on top of a past narrative, the past is very much alive in the streets of Oxford. 'If only you had come in June you may have seen Encaenia, the academic procession for honour degrees . . . it's the thing in all the postcards, with a pageboy carrying the chancellor's robe train and lots of pomp and circumstance.' This is a real thing, not historical re-enactment, a bona fide event with meaning and significance that takes place every year. To those of us whose only experience of meaningful local events is the weekly cascade of police cars that file into town on a Friday night, the idea of Encaenia is both brilliant and bonkers. We walked

Below | Christchurch College, the filming location for many *Harry Potter* scenes.

through the idyllic streets and underneath the Venetian-inspired 'Bridge of Sighs', and heard the 'ping' of bicycle bells, as book-filled panniers pedalled past us. It really felt like we had entered a completely different world.

The earliest evidence of Oxford as a place of learning dates to the eleventh century. The colleges are the real drivers of the university; as a student your affiliation is to your college, not the university as a whole. But even if you are not a student or member of staff, the university calendar is still likely to affect you. Some businesses, such as Ceci's favourite sandwich shop, actually close during the summer because there's not enough trade to make opening viable. You may also decide to keep off the streets during the exam season too, for 'trashing' is commonplace. A relatively recent tradition, trashing is the art of simultaneously plying your friend with alcohol and covering them in some kind of celebratory confetti after they emerge from their final exam – baked beans, silly string, flour, eggs and buckets of water are all good options it seems.

The other thing that made Ceci's tour so special was that she had spent lots of time thinking about what *we* would be interested to see. *Harry Potter* filming locations were therefore high on the list of places we visited. Divinity Hall at the Bodleian Library was used as the Hogwarts hospital wing in *The Philosopher's Stone*, and we even got to see the courtyard where Malfoy gets turned into a ferret by 'Mad-Eye' Moody in *The Prisoner of Azkaban*.

Even though we only had an hour Ceci made it count. We returned to the station with minutes to spare, only to find out our train had been cancelled! Nonetheless, if someone tells you Oxford cannot be done in an hour, they'd be right – unless that is you have Ceci, tour guide extraordinaire.

Knights in Shining Armour

Cerian, from Aberdare to Treherbert

Often, to save time when travelling, it can be more advantageous to connect between the end of two lines in a taxi or on a bus rather than doubling back on the train. This is a trick we learnt through the many Tube Challenges we've attempted over the years (but that's a story for another book).

Making connections between the ends of lines in the Welsh Valleys around Cardiff was always going to be a place where this would happen. There are six Valley Lines in total, all linked to either Cardiff Central/Caerdydd Canolog or Cardiff Queen Street/Caerdydd Heol y Frenhines stations. The connection between Rhymney/Rhymni and Ebbw Vale Parkway/Parcffordd Glyn Ebwy can be done by catching the No. 20 and then E11 buses (with a mini walk in between the two).

The plan for getting between Aberdare/Aberdâr and Treherbert was still up in the air on the morning of our visit. We simply thought we'd figure out a bus or taxi when we got there. That is until our friend Ruth alerted us to a message on Facebook: 'There's a lady offering you a lift . . . and she sounds nice and normal too' (this wasn't always the case). But would just a few hours be enough notice to meet with

'Rydyn ni'n caru Cymru!'

this mystery saviour? It felt like a bit of a long shot to us, but almost instantly there was a reply: 'No problem I'll be at the station . . .' And just like that, our connection was sorted.

As the train doors opened Cerian was waiting to greet us as promised, arms wide open with a huge 'Welcome to Aberdare!' hug. She'd even bought us a bottle of champagne. It was at this moment we realised we officially love Wales. *Rydyn ni'n caru Cymru!*

Cerian drove us along the Rhigos Road, which twists and turns through the valley and up to Craig y Llyn with its incredible panoramic views. It is the highest point within this part of the Valleys, almost 600 metres (2,000 feet) above sea level, and as well as showing off the phenomenal natural landscape it also reveals some of the area's mining history too. Looking out across the valley you can see the Tower Colliery, the longest-operational deep-level mine in the country, which ran from 1864 until 2008. It tells a powerful story of the spirit of the local mining community, who defied all odds to remain open long after the majority of other mines closed. Its success was due to the coming together of the miners and their families, 239 of whom contributed a share of their 1994 redundancy money to buy out and run the business themselves.

Abandoned for just over a decade there is now an ambition to clean up the colliery site and restore it to its former glory. Whether as a museum, visitor attraction or some other kind of business is not yet clear – the primary focus is simply to ensure the memory of those who fought for and worked the site does not dissolve to nothing.

Below | Craig y Llyn. In the right foreground of the picture you can see Tower Colliery, which was bought by workers and remained open until 2008.

This spirit of togetherness and community remains strong in the Valleys. Cerian told us about a choir and music festival organised by herself and other local people, The Glam. Created in response to the government funding cuts for the arts, The Glam tackles the shortage of music provision in schools by offering classes, and every year there is a festival to celebrate the achievements of everyone who has taken part. Cerian is not just *our* knight in shining armour.

'This one was completely unintentional'

Louise and Matthew in Thorne

The town of Thorne in South Yorkshire greedily has two stations: Thorne South, situated on the line that goes down the right-hand side of the River Humber to Grimsby and Cleethorpes, and Thorne North, on the line to the left of the river up to Hull. Both are just a few stops from Doncaster.

According to Google it takes approximately 25 minutes to walk between the two stations. A leisurely stroll through the town, we thought, with hopefully a glimpse of the Thorne miniature railway and maybe even a detour to the wonderfully historic parish church (taking in the remains of Peel Hill castle seemed too much to ask for in such a short space of time). After about 15 minutes, however, we started to get a feeling that we might not even make our connecting train. 'This could be bad,' said Geoff, as we started to pick up the pace. 'I think we might have miscalculated it.'

Suddenly a car pulled up beside us. 'Are you Geoff and Vicki?' a voice from inside the car called. 'Do you need a lift?!'

While our sound advice is always *not* to get in a car with complete strangers, the public nature of our adventure had brought us close to so many people we had never met before with positive consequences, and in this instance we felt confident that this was no exception to the rule.

Geoff: If neither of us believed in fate before now, we were strident converts in this moment. The minute we needed a lift, someone turned up to give us one. Absolutely unbelievable.

The people in the car turned out to be Louise and Matthew. They lived in Thorne and had been driving home from the butcher's (ah, how Yorkshire life differs from London living) when they spotted us. According to our rescuers it usually takes about 40 minutes to walk from the one Thorne station to the another, which means two things: Google Maps was wrong (horror!), and we would have missed our connection if they hadn't been driving past.

Above | Leaving Thorne South station, on the branch south of the River Humber towards Grimsby and Cleethorpes.

As a town, Thorne is unassuming but the fact it has two stations tells you something about the busyness of the area. The difference between Thorne North and South lies predominately with passenger numbers. As locals, it was Matthew and Louise's impression that Thorne South gets more passengers because it is more residential and further from the convenience of the motorway. Interestingly the statistics show that Thorne North is the more popular. Weirdly they both receive relatively similar services, once an hour in either direction, so perhaps it is to do with their destinations. Would it seem reasonable to assume that Hull is ultimately more popular than Grimsby or Cleethorpes? It was the 2017 UK City of Culture after all, and that is hard to beat.

It seemed unfair that almost as soon as we had met Matthew and Louise we were saying goodbye. Unlike many of our other encounters, this was completely unintentional and unplanned. While this wasn't the only place that coincidences of this nature occurred, the kindness of strangers never held greater meaning than it did on the road to Thorne North.

Staff

Ian the Selfie King of Lancaster station

Geoff: *When we get to Lancaster, there's this guy called Ian. He takes selfies with people and he wants to meet us.*

   Vicki: *OK, cool.*

   Geoff: *No, you don't understand, he takes selfies. It's his thing. He's the selfie king.*

   Vicki: (Short laugh) *OK, he wants to grab a selfie with us.*

   Geoff: *No, he is literally the selfie king. That's his name. His name on Twitter. He is the selfie king. Ian the selfie king. Everyone knows him.*

   Vicki: (More slowly) *OK . . .*

Lancaster is a key station along the West Coast Main Line and welcomes over 2 million people every year. It feels like you can get a train to almost anywhere from here – up to Carlisle and Glasgow, down to Crewe, Birmingham and London. Multiple train operating companies run services from the station, but the building is staffed and managed by Virgin Trains. And we challenge you to find a more hospitable welcome from a Virgin team member than we received from Ian.

   Ian's exuberance makes him an absolute joy to talk to. He has worked at Lancaster for over 20 years and it's clear that he loves his job. As busy a station as Lancaster is, Ian takes it all in his stride – dispatching trains, supporting the team and dealing with customer enquiries with flare and ease. The selfie thing just evolved it seems, and now Ian has become well known for it. Virgin Trains have even run competitions providing first class tickets to those who take the best selfie with Ian. Staff, passengers, trains, animals and celebrities alike, Ian will take a selfie with one and all.

   Ian asked if Vicki would like to make the station announcement.

   Vicki: *Would I like to make a station announcement? Honestly, I don't think I've ever said yes to anything so quickly in my entire life!*

   The announcement was for the train we were about to board, the 12.26 to Heysham Port. Except, the dot matrix sign said Heysham Harbour. Wait. There's no Heysham Harbour station, only Heysham Port! A little flummoxed, Vicki carried on but announced Heysham Port

'Have we got time for a selfie?'

Time Destination   Expected
12:26 Heysham Harbour   On Time

Calling at: :ambe and Heysham Harbour.

Operated by northern

12 25 02

Above | Heysham hiccup. The dot matrix display at Lancaster displays Heysham Harbour rather than Heysham Port.

rather than Harbour. Ian shook Vicki's hand, said thank you and congratulated her on a job well done (though we did notice a few seconds later he put out a second announcement for the 'Harbour' train). Heysham Harbour was the original name of the station when it opened in the early nineteenth century, but it hasn't been known as this since the 1970s. No one we've spoken to since has been able to explain this dot matrix anomaly.

While this encounter with Ian was only brief, by chance, on the way back through Lancaster later that day, we met again. This time, Ian took us over to the station's now abandoned and disused Platform 6.

'We don't want to take you away from what you're supposed to be doing,' we said, as Ian unlocked a heavy-looking door and led us into a series of abandoned stairwells and corridors. But Ian is proud of Lancaster and wanted to share its delights with us.

For us, Ian is the epitome of the railways. He puts people first and provides a service that makes their day better – he certainly did that for us. If they don't erect a blue plaque in his honour when he retires, we're going to have to have some serious words with someone. Or at least post a protest selfie online.

Settle–Carlisle team

'Oh it's you,' said a gentleman in a Northern uniform, as we wandered around the very quaint Appleby station. 'We were wondering when you might come by. Let me get Anne, she'd love to meet you.'

Anne is operations manager for the Settle–Carlisle Railway Development Company (which is different from the Friends of the Settle–Carlisle Line and the Settle and Carlisle Railway Trust; honestly, how many organisations does one line need?). Railway development companies are increasingly common across the country, but are not often well known except in the specific areas they operate. They function to support specific lines, promoting services and working closely with communities around the stations. Anne's office is based at Appleby but her role covers the entire line. She manages the refreshment trolleys on the trains (which serve a mean cup of tea), staff in the booking offices at Appleby and Settle, and carries out promotion and social media for the company.

'The railway provides a lifeline to many'

The first thing Anne did was to offer us a tea and a snack (maximum points for hospitality). One of the many priorities of the development company is to support local businesses and all the snacks on offer were locally sourced. We can verify it was one of the best cherry flapjacks we'd ever eaten!

Anne and Manny (the Northern-clad member of staff mentioned above) were incredibly knowledgeable and super friendly. They demonstrated a real passion for their work and a belief wholeheartedly in the importance of the railways and the invaluable service they provide to local people. In these parts of Cumbria's Eden Valley and the Yorkshire Dales there are no regular bus routes, so smaller villages and towns can become easily isolated. As such, the railway provides a lifeline to many. Anne talked about how ideally the line could have more services, particularly earlier in the morning and later on in the evening, to support local commuting.

Above | Appleby station, maximum quaint!

While more passengers is always ideal, Appleby and the other Settle–Carlisle stations do see a steady flow of visitors during the summer, when train excursions and rambles through the Dales reach their peak. Sometimes trains are delayed as it can take up to five minutes to get everyone from a tour group on or off the train. There's just no accounting for people in the timetable.

Besides the attractions of the trains and a good ramble, local towns and villages also offer unique days out, and this is something Anne and her team are keen to promote. Just ten minutes' walk from the station, for example, is the town of Appleby-in-Westmorland itself, a market town that has retained many of its historical features. At one end of the main street is Appleby Castle and at the other is St Lawrence's Church, a Grade I listed building. Both were heavily influenced by notable noble Lady Anne Clifford, High Sheriff of Westmorland, during the seventeenth century. The town is picture perfect, and the only thing likely to hold up the traffic (except the annual Appleby Horse Fair) is a family of ducks waddling unconcerned in the middle of the road.

The Campaigners

Pilning Station Group

If you've ever caught a train from London to Cardiff, then you've passed through, at high speed, one of Britain's most intriguing and least-used stations: Pilning (mentioned briefly in Chapter 1). Located near Severn Beach, Pilning used to have a regular daily train service. In fact, Pilning village was once served by two stations, the other being on a branch which didn't cross the River Severn. By the 1980s the service had been cut back to just one train a day in each direction, which only called during daylight hours because the station lighting had been disconnected. Interestingly, a similar scenario occurs at Falls of Cruachan station in Scotland, where due to lack of lighting trains only stop during the summer months. (Ironic, given that it is the nearest station for visiting the Hollow Mountain – a power station built inside Ben Cruachan.)

By 2006 the service was reduced even further to just two trains a week, one going west, one going east. Surely it can't get any worse, right? Wrong. In 2016, due to the electrification scheme taking place along the line between Bristol and South Wales, the footbridge at the station was removed to make way for the overhead cabling. It was never put back, cutting off access to the westbound platform and making westbound trains impossible to catch (or alight from). As compensation, the station does now get an additional eastbound service (that's two services a week in the same direction) and a special 'fares easement' is in place. This means you can buy a ticket for a westbound destination, and the cost of travelling east first to change at Patchway or Filton Abbey Wood stations is waived.

But the locals aren't giving up. Resident Jonathan King originally started a campaign to improve the service in the 1980s; today that campaign is known as the Pilning Station Group. A few weeks before we got there, we were contacted by active group member Olga, who was very keen to meet us and share the story of their ongoing railway struggles.

Without catching the train, the only way to get to Pilning is by car and Olga very kindly picked us up from Severn Beach station, about three or so miles away, where there is also a cracking view of the Severn Bridge.

One of the first things you'll notice is that there is no classic 'double arrow' logo sign by the nondescript road that leads up to Pilning station. The station itself has been slowly run down over the years, and with all the electrification work taking place it is essentially a building site. A country lane leading up to the platform, no lighting, no buildings, no ticket machines, no car park and no footbridge.

At the time we visited, a big part of the group's campaign was a competition they'd devised called the Pilning Grand Slam. The rules were thus: catch the first train of the day (around 8 a.m.) and see how many other services you could travel on before returning to Pilning on the lunchtime train. Then GWR changed the train times, and so a new game has now been created, the Pilning Scramble. The rules here are to catch the morning service from Pilning and stop at as many stations as possible before travelling back on the afternoon train. You score points (as per Scrabble) for the first letter of the name of each of the stations you've stopped at.

'The Pilning Scramble'

Olga is an inspiration. Committed, enthusiastic, determined, creative and passionate. Take a look at the group's website and you'll see an unlimited number of ways you can support the campaign and get involved. It doesn't matter how local or not you may be. Olga even created a 'Song for Pilning' complete with accompanying YouTube video.

Through Olga and the group's tenacity the awareness of Pilning's plight continues to grow. On the last Sunday in August 2017, GWR even stopped an additional service at the station. Olga organised 25 people to take the train, though we're not sure how they all got home again as there was no returning service. Hopefully they've made their way back by now.

We hope the future for Pilning includes many more stopping services, perhaps even enough to warrant a change of name. Olga suggested Pilning Parkway. 'You can get the train from here to Bristol and avoid all the congestion on the roads!'

Below | The westbound platform at Pilning, abandoned and becoming overgrown.

Friends of Reddish South Station

While we will always advocate for increased passenger services, even to some of the country's most remote stations (our philosophy being 'build it and they will come'), it is theoretically understandable why some stations receive only a few scheduled stops each week. Berney Arms (see page 132) is arguably a good case in point. For other stations, however, it just baffles us as to why they are served so poorly. The line from Stockport to Stalybridge is one such example.

There has been only one train a week along this line since the early 1990s, despite rigorous campaigning. That's over 25 years that those who live closest to Reddish South or Denton stations have had to travel to an alternative station to make their way into Manchester. And for anyone wanting to go to Huddersfield, Leeds or beyond this often means catching a train travelling in the opposite direction before

making an appropriate connection. Or at least waiting until the weekly train, which during our adventure was on a Friday morning.

On the day we journeyed the line we boarded at Reddish South, deliberately to meet with the Friends of Reddish South Station campaign group. There to tell us more about their work was Dave, Terry, Keith, Kim, Alan, Cyril, Christine and Barbara.

Over the years the service has been bounced around on different days; it used to be on a Saturday until it changed to the more awkward 9.27 a.m. slot on Friday. Awkward, because it's three minutes too early to apply Senior or other railcard discounts. Deliberate? Some of the Friends suspect it could be. We couldn't possibly comment.

Since our visit the service reverted to a Saturday, the upside being weekends are classified as off-peak so railcards are valid all day – hurrah! There has also been an increase in the number of services, from one to ... two. At 8.46 a.m. you can now catch the train from Stalybridge stopping at all stations to Stockport, then just 35 minutes later you can make the return trip. Just enough time for a mini explore.

'The resolve of the group will not be diminished'

Despite these changes, the Friends of Reddish South Station continue to rally for better provision and their resolve will not be diminished. Over the years they have worked hard to promote the station and the line through regular events and projects. In 2016 they won the Association of Community Rail Partnerships' Best Kept Station Award and received a highly commended at the beginning of 2018. Accolades well deserved. Once overgrown and unattractive, past projects have seen the installation of artwork and planting of gardens, which really bring the platforms to life in an otherwise heavily industrial area.

But what is the future for the Stockport to Stalybridge line? Will it forever be restricted to just one or two services a week? Will the station ever be given more priority or will the same struggles continue for another 25 years? It is unlikely that the line will ever be decommissioned – this takes an Act of Parliament which is a lengthy and expensive process. Services like this are known as a 'Parliamentary service' for this very reason. A weekly service is the minimum requirement to keep a line operational before an Act of Parliament is needed to retire it completely.

During our visit, more and more passengers got on as the train stopped at Denton and Guide Bridge. In fact, the statistics show that over the last two years footfall has more than doubled, from 34 to 98 passengers, a trend we and the Friends hope will continue.

Home from Home

Karen, Matlock Bath

Surprisingly, one of the most comforting feelings on a long railway journey is when you get to stay in a location for more than just one night. This means you can unpack and not have to almost instantly repack your bag again for the morning. For us, it also meant that we could think about looking for a place where we could wash and more excitingly dry our clothes.

'Understood our taste perfectly'

This was taken to a whole new level when we met Karen, who not only washed our clothes but hung them on her washing line (if you live in a city and don't have a garden you NEVER underestimate the scent of clothes dried on the line). Karen, who made us packed lunches so that we could have a break from processed railway station food. Karen, who invited us to stay in her home for two nights. Karen, who actually moved out of her home for two nights so that we could get comfortable and not feel under pressure to entertain her while we were there. Karen, who created for us a home from home.

And where does such a generous person live? Why Derbyshire of course. Karen's love of her community and for the whole of Derbyshire was infectious. And to be fair, it wasn't difficult to be infected.

Matlock Bath is home to the Heights of Abraham, right on the edge of the Peak District National Park. To reach the Heights you take our fourth favourite mode of transport, a cable car! And my goodness what a stunning view.

The scenery for us had double the impact because just a few hours before we had been in Lincolnshire, one of the flattest areas of the country. To have gone so quickly from one landscape to another was difficult to process, but emphasises one of the simplest pleasures of taking a railway adventure: the changing views outside the window. Next time you're on a train put that book down for five minutes (unless it's this one) and absorb the scenery. Before you know it you'll be somewhere that looks completely new.

Karen also reminded us that Derbyshire has a strong railway heritage. Just a short walk from Derby station itself and you'll find the Midland Railway Cottages, thought to be the earliest surviving purpose-built houses for railways workers. They form part of a Railway Conservation Area that includes the Brunswick Inn, one of two railway-themed pubs. The second is the Alexandra Hotel, a place we instantly fell in love with – every inch of the pub is covered in railway memorabilia; there is even half a diesel unit in the car park (we didn't even begin to ask how it got there). The best piece, however, was the 'train spotter' notice, which we couldn't resist taking a snap of. Karen had understood our taste perfectly.

Below | We kept telling people, we're not train spotters!

Brief Encounters

Steve at Berney Arms

As England's remotest station, Berney Arms is not a place that you'd expect to bump into anyone. And if you do, you certainly don't expect them to be the one exact person you need to speak to.

Berney Arms is a request stop in the middle of the Norfolk countryside. While once there were station buildings next to the platform that included a post office and a signal box, there is now just an open expanse of marshland. The marshland, however, is one of the most important in the country, home to thousands of wintering wildfowl, specifically over 15,000 pink-footed geese. Nature lovers come from all over the world for a ramble and to see these incredible creatures.

The station is named after one of the area's only remaining buildings, the nearby pub. In the past, the pub had been a commercial draw, bringing people to the area particularly during the summer months. In October 2015, The Berney Arms closed and in the following year the Save The Berney Arms campaign was launched. The campaign's aim was to crowdfund some of the costs to buy and renovate the pub, restoring it as a local hub. However, an internet search could not bring us up-to-date information, so as we alighted onto the station platform in May 2017 we were still wondering what the future fate of the pub might be.

Below | Berney Arms, literally in the middle of nowhere. Looking down the line.

Warning
Do not trespass
on the Railway
Penalty £1000

As we stood watching the train pull away we happened to turn and speak with one of the other passengers who had also just got off. His name was Steve and he was the treasurer of the Save The Berney Arms campaign. What are the chances!?

Steve told us that Save The Berney Arms had almost been successful in buying the property at auction earlier in the year, but that the owner had taken it off the market at the last moment. They were now in direct conversation with the owner about the possibilities of still acquiring the pub, their continuing hope being that they could create a renewed place for the community rather than let the building become a private home.

In the 1960s the population of Berney Arms was 18. Today that number is even lower. When you stand on the platform it really feels like the end of the line, even though technically it's in the middle.

Even here in the remotest of places, quite literally, it is humbling to realise there is no shortage of people who are willing to come together to preserve and improve opportunities for others and for future generations.

Strangers on the train, Scarborough to Bridlington

'On the train you never know who you might end up talking to'

On the train out of Scarborough we started to chat to a couple who sat across the aisle from us. Actually, we think they started the conversation, having asked if we were photographers – they'd clearly spotted all our camera equipment.

We briefly explained what we were doing and they asked where we were from. In exchange, as is the polite thing to do, we asked the same question back. They lived in Bridlington, just a couple of stops down the line and the same place we were headed, and told us they regularly got the train up to Scarborough to go to the arcades for a few hours. 'How often?' we asked. 'Most weeks,' they replied. We soon found ourselves dispensing advice on railcards. They didn't know about the Two-Together, and were interested to hear that they could be saving themselves a third on their travel tickets (see chapter 3).

Our lives, it quickly became apparent, were quite different. Geoff reacted with a little astonishment when they mentioned they'd never been to London before. 'Have you never wanted to go?' asked Geoff. 'No, not really,' came their reply. The notion that someone wouldn't want to visit London, the country's capital, seemed incomprehensible. But then, we reminded ourselves, we'd never been to Bridlington.

Then came a moment that we thought might derail (excuse the pun) the pleasantries. 'So how did you vote in the referendum then?' they asked. 'Errrrr . . .'

That particular conversation, we've noticed when travelling, can quickly become quite heated and uncomfortable. So ashamedly we ducked around the issue, but almost instantly regretted it.

This railway adventure we were on was a step beyond the realm of our ordinary lives. It took us to places we'd never seen before and introduced us to people we'd otherwise likely never meet. It opened our eyes to the circumstances, the challenges, the perceptions of people whose lives are dramatically different from our own. This is something only public transport can do. In a car you choose who sits in your passenger seat. On the train you never know who you might end up talking to and what you might discover about them and yourself.

As we continued our journey we lamented the lost opportunity to speak to them some more. This is probably one of the only regrets we have of our adventure. One day we hope to head back to Bridlington and finish that conversation.

Below | Bridlington station was a complete surprise to us. The incredible care taken by staff to look after hanging plants and the railway ephemera in the café is overwhelming.

The Gift Givers

Bernie, back in Lancaster

Gifts and souvenirs are a crucial part of any adventure. They are the talismans you take home which recall a place, a moment or a person that you encountered along the way. From cups of tea (we're still detoxing from all the caffeine) and snacks, to postcards, books and maps about the railways, to local delicacies like the mini bottle of gin infused with Yorkshire tea from David or the Dundee marmalade from Garry, we were overwhelmed by everyone's generosity throughout our adventure. There was one gift, however, that captured the entirety of our journey, and it was something that we weren't prepared for.

'You're going to want to meet him, trust me.' This was the message we got from Ruth, who you now know picked up a lot of message requests on our behalf. It wasn't always possible to squeeze everything in, but a gentleman called Bernie had got in touch saying that he had a gift for us. Could he deliver it in person?

We ended up meeting at Lancaster, home as you'll recall of the Selfie King. Having scanned the platforms for a few minutes we suddenly spotted a chap carrying a large package under his arm. Initially Bernie looked a little nervous, but he handed over the parcel saying simply, 'This is for you.'

'Some things just leave you speechless'

But there was nothing simple about this gift. A wooden, laser-cut, hand-painted, British Rail-style totem sign that said 'All The Stations'.

Some things just leave you speechless. All we could manage to blurt out was, 'Why have you done this?' 'Because I saw your story on the BBC and it made me smile,' was all Bernie replied.

Bernie is an artist and photographer and felt that a project such as ours warranted such a gift. We felt he could make a fortune selling these, but for Bernie the joy was in the one off. A real artist.

From our conversation we gathered that Bernie wasn't a prolific railway adventurer himself, but the spirit in which he had made this incredible gift encapsulated one of the overarching themes of our entire journey. The railways are nothing without people. Without their passion, their dedication, their individuality, their generosity to support others or to campaign for their communities, the railways truly wouldn't be what they are today. And if more people knew it, that five-minute delay to their morning commute may not seem like such a big deal. We are all, after all, only human.

LEAST-used stations by passenger usage (2016/17)

1 Barry Links – 24 passengers
2 Teesside Airport – 30 passengers
3 Breich – 48 passengers
4 Redcar British Steel – 50 passengers
5 Kildonan – 76 passengers
6 Reddish South – 94 passengers
7 Golf Street – 104 passengers
8 Havenhouse – 106 passengers
9 Buckenham – 122 passengers
10 Stanlow & Thornton – 128 passengers

Shippea Hill now in 14th place with 156 passengers (previously at no. 1 with 12). Coombe Junction Halt has jumped from 4th to 18th place with 212 passengers. Pilning has moved from 3rd to 20th place with 230 passengers. (All figures from the Office of Rail and Road.)

MOST-used station by passenger usage (2016/17)

1 London Waterloo (99.4 million)
2 London Victoria (75.8 million)
3 London Liverpool Street (67.3 million)
4 London Bridge (47.8 million)
5 London Euston (44 million)
6 Birmingham New Street (42.3 million)
7 Stratford (42.2 million)
8 London Paddington (35.8 million)
9 London King's Cross (33.8 million)
10 London St Pancras International (33.4 million)

CHAPTER 5

YOU CAN'T HELP BUT LOVE THE TRAINS

YOU CAN'T HELP BUT LOVE THE TRAINS

Railways are often seen as the territory of the train enthusiast – those who have encyclopaedic knowledge of the origins and history of the network and who can distinguish one class of train from another. We set out thinking it doesn't matter what class of train you're on, the point is you're on one.

Geoff: I did wonder though if, by the end of it all, we would have been on a least one of every type of rolling stock out there. There are 60 different classes of train in total, and the urge to know was too great, so later I made a log of everything we travelled on. I can tell you now . . . yes, we travelled on every different type of train except one, the Class 155.

That we started to become familiar with all the different types of train stock was perhaps inevitable, and there were some which we certainly felt more of an affinity to than others. As you'll find out, Vicki's affection for a classic Pacer was one of the ongoing controversies of the trip.

But more than simply just *knowing* what the different types of train are, there is something deeper that can be understood by identifying what kinds of trains are used where on the network. It seems obvious, but the larger, more modern and technologically capable trains are given the task of managing services over longer distances. They typically handle higher volumes of passengers and are frequent visitors to principal cities and towns across the country. It is fair to say that places like London, Birmingham, Manchester and Edinburgh get the majority of the best and most reliable trains.

More rural locations tend to get the smaller, older units, which is understandable in places where passenger numbers are much lower. However, there were some real surprises for us in busy locations like Lincoln and Ipswich, which we noticed also had to cope with smaller trains, even during peak commuting hours. It was these moments when knowing the type and age of the trains we were on seemed to speak volumes about the ongoing struggles faced by many train operating companies to manage demand in multiple locations across the country.

The reasons why it can be so difficult for companies to match the demand for services are complex and take us into the murky territory of discussing privatisation vs nationalisation – about which people have written entire books and still not come to an agreed consensus. But, in essence, it's important to remember that every train operating company functions as a franchise for a finite period of time, not the long term. A franchise is awarded by the Department for Transport (DfT) to the company who proposes the 'best' business plan at the time of tender. Once agreed this plan dictates the amount of money the company is granted – if they have said they'll spend x amount of money and use y number of trains, there will be no additional supplements from the DfT later on. Individual companies can decide to put in more of their own money, but what is their incentive if there is no guarantee they will continue to run the franchise at the end of their term? As a business, decisions are made that ensure the books balance, and that doesn't always equate to providing more or longer services, or even in some cases being able to match passenger demand. To see it from a purely operational perspective, the rail industry is one giant mathematical equation that everyone, all TOCs and government departments, is working hard to keep on track(!). We understand that there is not one easy answer.

But we digress. The names of the trains are just as complicated to fathom. Three quarters of the way through our trip we were lucky enough to be invited to take a look around Hitachi's manufacturing depot in Newton Aycliffe. At the time they were working on the construction of the new AT300 trains. Since our visit these trains are now known simultaneously by GWR as the Class 800 Intercity Express Train (IET) and by Virgin customers as the Azuma. So, already that's three different classifications for exactly the same type of train!

Maybe it's this complexity that makes being able to identify each individual train so appealing to so many. And we have to admit that there were moments when it was fun to try to guess what type might be coming around the corner – especially if we thought it might be a Pacer. Whether old or new, comfortable or not, loved or hated, we experienced them all (except the Class 155, bah!). So, in case you're similarly curious, here's a rundown of the most notable ones out there and some of their features. Notebooks and pens at the ready? It's the train section . . . let's go spotting!

'A proper train'

Class 37

The railway hugs the Cumbrian coastline looking out over the Irish Sea. Occasionally the idyllic sounds of the ocean, waves crashing against the shore and gulls cawing overhead, are interrupted by a noise so loud and so distinct that it gets its own name among the train enthusiast community. The 'Tractor' is officially known as a Class 37 and is what many people consider to be a 'proper train'.

Vicki: From the outset we received lots of comments from people instructing us on what is and isn't a 'proper train'. For someone like myself, who is not particularly drawn to the intricacies of train design, I was perplexed by the vehemence with which people debate why some trains are better than others. Geoff got really excited when he thought we would get the chance to travel on a Tractor, and I really wanted to understand why this was something so special.

For many, it seems, it's the nostalgia. A throwback to how services used to be. The Class 37 is a diesel locomotive, which means all the power is contained and controlled in one place, in the unit at the front of the train. All the passenger carriages behind are simply pulled along by the loco unit. There are no engines or mechanics under the carriages at all. Many think this makes for a better passenger experience, the ride is smoother, and it's less noisy (inside) and there's more room. It's these factors that constitute what some people, including Geoff, call a 'proper train'.

But these trains (sorry, locomotives) date back to the 1950s and 60s. What on earth are they still doing on the network today? The reason is that some train operating companies have reached capacity with their DMUs (diesel multiple units – where the engines are integrated into and underneath the passenger carriages), so resourcefully they have hired a number of Class 37s to fill in the gaps. We knew that we might get lucky with a Class 37 along the Cumbrian coast, but later we found out that Greater Anglia are doing the same thing on the lines between Norwich, Great Yarmouth and Lowestoft. The Fife Circle in Scotland (just north of Edinburgh) is another place where you might sometimes get loco-hauled services. It seems that despite the development of new technology, there is still a reliance on the mechanics of the past.

Due to their distinctive sound and shape, the Class 37 is infamous among train enthusiasts. If you plan ahead there is a way to know which services will be carried out by a Tractor, and that's the old-fashioned way: by looking at a printed pocket timetable – yes, they still exist! On Northern services, those operated by a Class 37 will be annotated with a special 'diamond' symbol.

If you do decide to hunt down one of these services, you'll likely not be the only one doing so. We discovered the Tractor actually attracts more than your regular commuter. They are extremely popular with enthusiasts who go out of their way specifically to ride them. So popular in fact that Northern were considering keeping them running longer than planned because they'd turned into something of an attraction in themselves.

They can be an attraction for staff, too. We got chatting to our guard Steve at Barrow station. Well, it was Steve who spotted us really. He said he had to come and talk to us because some of his colleagues had been discussing our adventure and lots of people considered that we weren't 'doing it properly' (some people thought we should be getting *out* at every station and waiting for the next service for our journey to really count). Despite this, however, Steve was keen to chat and told us that one of the things that drew him to working on the railways more than 30 years ago was engines like the Class 37. 'They're brilliant locomotives,' he said, with a definitive thumbs up.

They're *not* popular with everyone though. Members of Barrow Borough Council have declared them unreliable – there have been many instances of them breaking down along the line – and insist that they actually put some local passengers off travelling. Their notorious Tractor noise is also a big problem for some who live close to the line. Because of this, and other complaints, it is likely that the use of Class 37s in Cumbria will be phased out. Which makes us just a little bit sad, but not for the environment – which without these overpowered engines will be decidedly healthier and happier as a result.

Pacer

Now, we realise that Pacers are the Marmite of the railway world. You either love them or hate them so much you'd rather not travel at all. If you're a hater, please don't throw this book away just yet. Let us see if we can change your mind, or at least bring the word Pacer into the more tolerant quadrant of your heart. Ready? Then we shall begin.

Let's start with an explanation about what a Pacer actually is. It's true, they are essentially buses on rails. They have bus-style bodies and seating configurations, and concertina doors just like on a bus. They are lightweight, low-cost designs that were introduced 'temporarily' onto the network in the 1980s and were never intended to still be operable nearly 40 years later. There is a whole series within the Pacer 'class' – all 142, 143 and 144 trains are Pacer variants. Because they are lightweight and have simplistic structural designs, they are not the most comfortable when travelling along the modern network. They're not great at evening out the bumps in the tracks or taking corners, and they certainly won't win any prizes for stealth. In the same way that the Class 37 is known fondly for its tractor-like sound, the Pacer is cursed for the high-pitched screeching noise it makes when braking or taking corners, in fact pretty much at any time it's in motion.

'Nodding Donkeys'

Above | A classic Pacer, or what some like to call a Nodding Donkey.

We should also mention their many nicknames. Some people know them as Nodding Donkeys. In Scarborough the train crews refer to them as Spam Tins. Both names are self-explanatory.

One of their biggest drawbacks is that they are mostly inaccessible for wheelchair users or any passengers needing step-free assistance while travelling, and it is for this reason that by 2020 there will no longer be any of the current Pacer trains on the network. By this point, all trains will have to comply with the persons of reduced mobility technical specification for interoperability (PRM-TSI). Spanish manufactures CAF are in the process of building 98 new units to replace them as we type.

However, there is already one modified Pacer on the network and just by chance we happened to board it while travelling from Worksop to Sheffield. It's a Class 144 variant which has been upgraded with a step-free entrance, a passenger dot matrix display (the in-carriage electronic screen that scrolls through the destinations along the route), a toilet with an automated door and even Wi-Fi! 'The Wi-Fi doesn't always work though,' we were told by one of the train's regular passengers – they were right, it didn't.

We experienced our first Pacer on the line from Paignton to Dawlish and Exeter in Devon and then up along the Barnstaple branch. You'll also catch a Pacer or two in the Welsh Valleys and Lincolnshire, after which they predominately live and work in 'The North', that is to say counties including all the Yorkshires (all of them), Tyne & Wear, Merseyside, Lancashire, Cheshire and Durham. If you spend a day travelling on Northern trains it's most likely you'll be on a Pacer.

In these areas the tiny Pacer train traverses epic landscapes, linking towns, villages, hamlets and cities through valleys, across flats (a Pacer's preferred gradient), along coasts and over hills, connecting communities who might otherwise be disconnected to public transport.

Unlike other modern train units, the bus-like nature of Pacers makes them feel like a friendlier way to travel. The seating is open, so you can see other people, share moments, have conversations and generally just engage with your fellow passengers. It is the very sociable nature of Pacers that grew Vicki's affection for them. The windows are also wider and give you a great view of the scenery (if they're not covered in condensation). Sometimes it feels like trains try to make you forget that you're travelling on the railway at all – windows are tinted, high-backed chairs make you feel alone, you withdraw onto your phone or laptop and you forget about the world around you. Not so on a Pacer. You know you're on a train!

And we're not alone in our appreciation of the Pacer, which is nice to know. The Peak Pacer Preservation Society aims to buy one of the last Class 142s and preserve it. It's thought that the last of this variant will make its final journey on the network in December 2019, so if you haven't yet experienced the brilliance of a Pacer make sure to do it in the next few months – they won't be around forever.

Sprinter

'They pop up all over the place'

Any train whose identifying number starts with '15-' falls into the Sprinter category. People often ask us what our favourite type of train is and if you *really* had to pin Geoff down he would say either the Class 156 Super Sprinter or Class 158 Express Sprinter. But there is another Sprinter that captured both our imaginations, and that is the anomaly that we came to feel was synonymous with our trip around the country, the humble single unit, the Class 153.

They didn't start life as single-car units. Originally they were all Class 155 double-car units, but as a network cost-saving measure they were split in two and – hey presto! – double the amount of trains. (The end without a driver's cab had one put in, so that they could be driven in either direction, which consequently did reduce some of the passenger space.)

Class 153s pop up all over the place, and we dare say we may have ridden the majority of them. Trips include the day we spent on the amazing Heart of Wales line, the shuttle back and forth between Cardiff Queen Street and Cardiff Bay, the Liskeard to Looe branch in Cornwall, several in Norfolk on Greater Anglia services, including Norwich to Cromer, the Swindon to Westbury train and the Coventry to Nuneaton service. There were three occasions, however, which were most memorable.

The first was the Ipswich to Felix-stowe line in Suffolk. Trains run this route every hour, picking up and drop-ping off at three villages along the way. We travelled at peak commut-ing hour, 6 p.m. The train was packed, standing room only, and from what we could gather this was not an unusual occurrence.

Above | This 153 Sprinter was joined up with another class of train to make two carriages along the Falmouth branch in Cornwall.

A similar scenario occurred a couple of weeks later at Lincoln, on an East Midland train heading up to Market Rasen. This time platform staff were dutifully corralling passengers, helping them find the best place to stand on the platform, encouraging those with buggies to fold them down to ease boarding and passengers with rucksacks to take them off to create more standing space inside. With just two single doors at either end of the one-car unit, if there's a lot of people get-ting on and off time can be lost, with knock-on effects to the schedule later down the line.

The final occasion was the most surprising, and that was on the ser-vice from Brighouse, through Halifax and Bradford where it reverses to Leeds, all on a single-car 153! Again, the train was unsurprisingly *heaving.*

Geoff: I remember thinking that this isn't a rural branch line. Halifax, Bradford, Leeds – these are all big towns and cities. How on earth can they justify running a one-car train here?

People outside of London often chastise the South East for having all the money for new trains and services. And yes, when you're on a tiny train through major conurbations in the north of England, you get an immediate appreciation for why they say that. If we could offer a list of recommendations to the powers that be, one of them would be to consider increasing seat numbers in areas that desperately need something better. Specifically starting with that Bradford train.

Moquette

We realise that this isn't technically a 'train', but it is a very distinctive train feature that we think deserves a section all of its own – we hope you'll us indulgence just this once.

Moquette is the word used to describe the seating fabric you find in almost all trains on the British network. It's a word derived from the French for 'carpet' due to the compactness of the fabric weave and the dense material used – it is, just like a carpet, tough and durable. Probably the most iconic and well known is the patterned moquette that features on the London Underground, but the big trains have them too.

As we travelled between different train operating companies we noticed that each train not only sported the brand and livery of that company on the outside (to help you know which train you're catching), but they also incorporated the colours and logos on the inside through the patterns on seats.

From day one, we knew this was something we should capture. With company franchises changing all the time, it's likely that some of the moquette we witnessed in 2017 will have completely disappeared in just a few years.

Apart from aesthetics, though, why and how is moquette important? Firstly, there's an impact on behaviour. If you've travelled on trains outside of Britain you may have experienced the more utilitarian design features, like on the New York City Subway. On the one hand this makes cleaning away any graffiti or vandalism easier, but it also creates a more sterile environment which people are less likely to preserve. With upholstered surroundings you create a completely different setting for passengers, a more curated and comfortable space that people will feel differently towards and hopefully respect.

'Take a second
to look at what
you're sitting
on'

Comfort is also a consideration: softer, warmer interiors give a more pleasant experience – good for passengers, good for business.

But the design itself is probably the most important aspect of any decent moquette. It reflects the train operating company and the area in which the train runs, and passengers really respond to it. We've heard of children who make up ice-cream flavours based upon the colours and patterns of the seats – genius!

The artists take a lot of time to create something that works for the train operating company and the routes served, producing memorable designs that match a particular ethos while not being too overwhelming in the space. It's a hard task.

Harriet Wallace-Jones and Emma Sewell of Wallace Sewell are perhaps the best-known moquette designers in Britain today. They have a

background in textile design for fashion and the home, and have often described the challenges of adapting their work to meet requirements for the travel industry. 'The designs had to be created using a very tight four-colour palette, briefed by TfL, and we utilised colour theory to make it appear that there are more than the given four colours.' Their patterns are seen and used by millions of people every year on the London Underground and Overground and they have now created moquette for Crossrail's new Elizabeth line.

The next time you get on a train make sure you take a second look at what you're sitting on. Some of the designs we saw, it has to be said, are pretty dull. But after much consideration, here in picture form are our top ten British railway moquette. Can you tell from the pictures which train operating companies they belong to? (Answers on page 158.)

Parry People Mover

On the line heading south-west out of Birmingham Snow Hill station you'll find Stourbridge Junction. Opened in the mid-nineteenth century, it is situated more than a mile outside of Stourbridge town centre, and it didn't take long before Stourbridge Town station was also built much closer to all the action.

Today a ten-minute shuttle service (fifteen minutes on a Sunday) operates between the two Stourbridge stations, which is serviced by the most unique class of train in the entire country – a Class 139 Parry People Mover, or as Vicki likes to describe it, 'The cutest train I've ever seen!'

There are only two Class 139 trains in Britain and both of them serve this branch line. The train itself is extremely environmentally friendly – it uses a flywheel to store energy from the train when it brakes going downhill, and then utilises that energy to power the train going back up. This makes it cheap and easy to maintain. There are always two members of staff on board, the driver and the guard, who swap roles periodically throughout their shift.

As a passenger, one of the best things about the train is that you have a clear view of the driver and the cab, so you can see everything going on in front – just as if you were driving the train yourself!

It is a tiny train, but because of the very short distance it has to travel there is a high frequency of services, so if you can't get on the first train that comes along it's only ten minutes until the next. This is a great example of cost, efficiency and environmental concerns all magically aligning to provide the perfect solution to the question of, 'How can we quickly and efficiently move lots of people a very short distance?'

If you ever get the chance take a ride on the Parry People Mover, you'll love the novelty. And if your guard is a tall gentleman who answers to the name of Phil, tell him we said hello!

1938 Stock

It's not unusual for train operating companies to utilise old train stock; the Class 37 is a perfect example of how past vehicles can help meet current network demands. To reuse stock that was never intended to run on the main line, however, and for that stock to be reaching its eightieth year in operation, is unique to the Isle of Wight.

The London Underground 1938 Tube stock was the most innovative underground rail stock available when it was launched in, well, 1938. It was the first London Underground train where all the engine and mechanical aspects of the vehicle were housed underneath the carriages, enabling increased passenger capacity. The London Transport Museum has a four-carriage unit which is cared for as a historic collection item, and yet on the Isle of Wight it is the standard running unit servicing the line come rain or shine. It has done since the 1990s. The island's Ryde Tunnel – where part of the line goes into an Underground-shaped tunnel – is the primary reason why this kind of train is most suitable here, as only a smaller vehicle can fit safely through it.

Brilliantly, the trains have retained many of their Underground features, such as the moquette. The carriage we travelled in was sporting the retro Metropolitan line design from the mid-1990s (trust us, it's exciting). If you find yourself at the guard end of the carriage, you might be able to pull down the foldaway guard seat to check what additional moquette might be hiding there – ours had a Network SouthEast design. Sneaky!

Another echo of the train's original purpose is in the line diagrams displayed inside the carriages. On the Underground you have a diagram of all the stations along the particular line you're travelling – these carriages have adapted the same principle for the Island Line stations.

There is a guard checking tickets on board, and whose job it also is to operate the passenger doors via the original guard's control panel inside the carriages. The one downside to such a nostalgic vehicle is the lack of modern suspension. It takes just 25 minutes to journey from one end of the line to the other, but it feels dramatically longer as it is SO rough and bumpy. And the noise! We could hardly hear Vicki's screams of delight at the moquette as we hurtled along the line from one station to the next. It does feel a bit like a roller-coaster ride, which you might either find highly enjoyable or terrifying. It borders a bit between the two – we'll leave you to decide for yourselves which camp you fall in.

Like Pacer trains, their time is coming to an end as they become increasingly unreliable and the parts to fix them harder to source. It's likely they'll be replaced by 2020, so if you've never been, go. Go now, while you can!

The railway on the Isle of Wight screams nostalgia which is, as Vicki says, enjoyably quaint. But how much does this antiquated system tell you about the island itself? With more time, we would have ventured beyond the boundaries of the stations to get more of a sense of the surrounding towns and villages and how they are supported

Above | The Isle of Wight Steam Railway runs trains to four stations starting at Smallbrook Junction and finishing at Wootton. Havenstreet station boasts a museum, visitor centre, refreshments and the Haven Falconry.

by the rail network, or lack of it. The existing line only runs part-way down the east coast of the island, which left us wondering about everywhere else.

But if like us you're short on time, you can travel even further back than the 1930s by picking up the Isle of Wight Steam Railway, on an adjacent platform at Smallbrook Junction (an infrequent stop on the line so do check the timetable). Though, ironically, many of the steam trains that run here are actually younger than the 1938 stock itself!

Steam

There are lots of nostalgic aspects to the modern British rail network – semaphore signalling, manual crossing barriers, heritage signage and lever frame signal boxes, to name just a few. But for some there is of course nothing more evocative than seeing a fully fledged steam engine puffing its way along the tracks.

Despite the lure of the past, we were adamant we would not get caught up in the world of heritage railways. Our adventure was to experience the *modern* network, to visit existing stations and find out how passengers travel and experience Britain's railways *today*. What we weren't expecting was for steam to be an active part of that story, and in a number of different ways.

ROYAL SCOT

PRIOR TO CONVERSION
THIS LOCOMOTIVE WITH THE ROYAL SCOT TRAIN WAS EXHIBITED AT THE CENTURY OF PROGRESS
EXPOSITION, CHICAGO, 1933, AND MADE A TOUR OF THE DOMINION OF CANADA AND THE UNITED
STATES OF AMERICA. THE ENGINE AND TRAIN COVERED 11,194 MILES OVER THE RAILROADS
OF THE NORTH AMERICAN CONTINENT AND WAS INSPECTED BY 3021601 PEOPLE.
W. GILBERTSON. — DRIVER.   T. BLACKETT. — FIREMAN.
J. JACKSON. — FIREMAN.   W. C. WOODS. — FITTER.

Below | *The Royal Scot,* steaming and ready to go at Penzance station.

On the morning of the first day of our adventure our path crossed with a chartered steam train at Penzance station. In actual fact, as we took a stroll around the town the night before we both looked at each other and inhaled a very smoky atmosphere. 'Is that a steam train?' we said. The smell is very distinctive – if you've never experienced it before, you are most definitely missing out.

These special excursion or chartered trains, as they are known, are run by private operating companies who offer tours and experiences, at a price, all over the country. And while the engines give passengers and onlookers a sense of the railway's past, a lot of additional equipment and adaptations have to be made to the train – to prove that they are compliant with modern safety standards – before they can even set a wheel on the tracks.

'We found the age of steam sneaking up all over the place'

One of the most famous chartered services is *The Jacobite*, operated by West Coast Railways, which runs between Fort William and Mallaig in Scotland. It's also known as the Harry Potter train as it crosses the Glenfinnan Viaduct, the iconic location for the filming of the *Hogwarts Express* for the *Harry Potter* movies. Of course we had to take a slight detour to capture a glimpse of *The Jacobite* in action, and unsurprisingly we weren't the only ones doing the same thing.

Geoff: People ask us why we didn't take The Jacobite *as part of our trip. The answer is simple: it doesn't stop at all the stations along the line.*

Chartered trains run in between and around the scheduled timetables of the main train operating companies and are given low priority on the lines, meaning they can often be delayed. And if a chartered train breaks down en route it impacts on the main-line passenger services. This is why you'll sometimes see chartered services with two engines. The idyllic steam engine at the front (the one everyone has paid to travel by), and a back-up diesel engine on the back which can push the train if required.

The second way that steam is integrated into the modern network can be seen where heritage lines offer convenient connecting services in-between lines. The best example of this is the Ffestiniog Railway in North Wales, where just a short distance from Porthmadog station is Porthmadog Harbour station and a regular service of magnificent steam engines that pull you all the way to Blaenau Ffestiniog – the start of the National Rail line up to Llandudno, approximately one hour and fifteen minutes via some spectacular Welsh scenery you'd otherwise not get the chance to witness.

The third, and most surprising, relationship that the railways have with steam is where you can actually pick up a steam train as part of a regular service between operating stations. The only example of this that we know of is in the north-east, from Whitby to Grosmont, where the North Yorkshire Moors Railway (NYMR) run a steam engine throughout the year. (Note that the train doesn't stop at any of the stations in between.) To continue from Grosmont station along the regular main line you have to change trains and skip across to the other platforms, else risk getting whisked off along the rest of the heritage route. Nonetheless, if the times match up this is a legitimate and impressive way to travel part of your commute. (The NYMR timetable changes regularly throughout the year, so make sure you check it before heading out.)

Above | The NYMR side of Grosmont station is a railway adventurers dream – all the heritage!

There are lots of other examples where heritage lines are connected via proximity to main-line stations. At Aviemore station, for example, simply walk across the passenger footbridge from Platform 1 to 2 and join the Strathspey Railway for a trip into the remote Scottish Highlands. And in Sussex, you can walk the few hundred yards from East Grinstead station to the Bluebell Railway for an equally brilliant experience along this heritage line to Sheffield Park (not actually in Sheffield, confusingly). There's also the Spa Valley Railway between Tunbridge Wells West and Eridge. It doesn't share the main-line railway tracks, but trains do share the island platform with regular services at Eridge station.

In the middle of our trip, the Swanage Heritage Railway also opened, running heritage services between Wareham, through Corfe Castle station and down to Swanage. Again, they share the platforms of the main-line station at Wareham. Initially they were running diesel engines only, but steam should be coming soon. Toot toot!

We found the age of steam sneaking up all over the place on our travels, and its popularity and the excitement of the passengers told us that steam is very much still part of the network. When you're out on the railways having your own adventure, why not look for some steam as part of your day – it'll be easier than you think.

All The Platforms (part one)

Shortest: Beauly (Scotland), 15.6 metres (51 feet)

Longest: Gloucester, 602.68 metres (1,977 feet)

Highest: Corrour, 411.48 metres above sea level (1,350 feet)

Lowest: Ryde Pier Head, 0 metres above sea level (0 feet)

Busiest: Clapham Junction (sees approximately 2,000 trains per day pass through, with interchanges accounting for 40 per cent of activities at the station)

Most decorated: Montpelier (*below*)

Furthest north: Thurso

Furthest south: Penzance

Furthest east: Lowestoft

Furthest west: Arisaig

All The Platforms (part two)

Stations with the most platforms on the network.

1   Birmingham New Street – 25 (due to a and b platform variants)
2   London Waterloo – 24
3   London Victoria – 19
4   Edinburgh Waverley – 18
5   London Euston – 18
6   Glasgow Central – 17
7   Leeds – 17
8   Manchester Piccadilly – 16
9   Reading – 15
10 St Pancras International – 15

Answers:
Top ten British railway moquettes
1 London Midland; **2** ScotRail; **3** TfL Rail / Crossrail; **4** Merseyrail; **5** Arriva Trains Wales; **6** TPE; **7** First Great Western; **8** Heathrow Connect; **9** Northern (newer one); **10** East Midlands

HAVE YOUR OWN
ADVENTURE

Journeying to All The Stations took us to places we'd never before visited and parts of the network we'd never before travelled; it led us to uncover the stories of communities, individuals and histories that have been – and continue to be – shaped and inspired by the railways. It took us off the beaten track, to the different, the unique and the curious. Travelling by train, however far you go, can encompass so much more than just the miles that you travel; it's not just a journey but an adventure.

So, are you up for a bit of a railway adventure of your own? Yes? Excellent.

There is almost nowhere we wouldn't recommend going, but having taken what we consider to be the most important railway ingredients – wonderful places to explore, quaint stations to alight at, people to talk to, trains to ride and the network to navigate – we've come up with five ultimate adventure routes for you to try.

For each route, it's best to do your own research to find out the most up-to-date timetabling and ticketing information (remember prices go up every year!), and to ensure station access and services haven't change dramatically from the time of writing this book.

If you take a family member, friend, your next-door neighbour or your significant other, you can share the experience and save money on tickets (see chapter 3). Or maybe you fancy the peace of solo travel. There's no wrong way to do it. Perhaps the greatest thing about rail travel is the freedom you have to experiment. If you like the sound of the next station along the route, why not get out and see what's there? (Of course, make sure there's another train you can catch when you want to get back on the move.) Or why not spontaneously get out one station early and walk the last part to your destination?

The second greatest thing about the railways is the opportunity it gives you to take in your surroundings and see things from a new perspective. In a car, you have to concentrate on the road ahead, and as a passenger you can often see only the hard shoulder or a hedge-row. A railway adventure means meandering through the landscape, over bridges, under rivers, through and around hills, above streets, by the sea, and sometimes out at sea (if you venture as far as the Isle of Wight), alongside farms, lochs and even nuclear power stations. You'll go from marsh to dales, from hills to shoreline, without lifting a finger. All you have to do is enjoy.

As well as invoking a sense of adventure, the other great ingredient for a successful trip is efficient packing. We recommend taking:

- ✓ An up-to-date timetable of the route you're travelling (you can download the latest PDF to your smartphone).
- ✓ A flask of tea (other beverages are available).
- ✓ Sandwiches and snacks.
- ✓ A camera.
- ✓ A fully charged phone (and portable charger, just in case).
- ✓ Emergency taxi money (there might be a castle just out of walking distance).
- ✓ A few conversation starters to get the ball rolling with the guard and passengers. Try 'Do you know the best way to get to x or y?' or 'Do you know the area well? We're/I'm trying to get to . . .' In Wales we found 'Can you speak Welsh?' was always a good opener.
- ✓ Pen and paper (for writing down the name of that sandwich shop the guard recommends).

And lastly, let us know how you get on. Share your adventures with us online with #HaveAnAdventure.

TO THE TRAINS!

Cambrian Line

Shrewsbury – Aberystwyth – Dovey Junction – Porthmadog

Train operating company: Arriva Trains Wales
Class of train: 158 Express Sprinter
Wi-Fi: Yes
Trolley service: No
Friendly guards: Yes!
Views: Scenic landscapes
Ticket options: Single off-peak tickets are reasonably priced here. However, if you're thinking of spending several days out and about, take a look at the Explore Wales Pass, which allows four days' travel over an eight-day period.

In summary: You can do the whole line in just one day – the views alone are worth the trip, even if you don't get out to explore any of the stations or locations along the way. However, as you know, we highly recommend planning in some time to stop and enjoy nearby points of interest. You can make this a two or even three-day adventure.

Shrewsbury

Shrewsbury station is deceptive. From the inside, you feel like you're walking around an average medium-sized station. There are five physical platforms, two of which are split into 'a' and 'b' ends, creating seven platform locations for trains. Facilities are ample and functional, they include a Pumpkin Café, a Starbucks and toilets. There are a few original British Rail benches, but it's not until you reach the ticket office with its quaintly tiled floor that you start to realise there might be something a bit special awaiting you outside. As you exit the station take a few moments to look back and be amazed by the Grade II listed structure that greets your eyes.

As well as the spectacular exterior of the station, the town of Shrewsbury has many interesting points of interest to offer. Firstly, there's the

Above | Shrewsbury station makes an impressive entrance. Built in 1849 by Thomas Penson Junior.

castle, just 30 seconds' walk from the station. Today the castle is home to the Shropshire Regimental Museum Trust and some immaculately landscaped grounds. There is also the town's connection to Charles Darwin. Darwin was born and lived here for many years and you can discover all his local associations by following the Darwin Trail – download from the Discover Darwin website.

Newtown/Drenewydd (Powys)

Look out for the great artwork on the platform at Newtown, created by young people from the area.

Caersws

Caersws station once appeared in an episode of the *Teletubbies*, where a family explored how to make their way across the level crossing safely. The episode (which is on YouTube) shows the crossing as manually operated, though today it is all on an automated system.

Machynlleth

The train divides at Machynlleth, so it's best to check that you are in the right carriage to carry on to Aberystwyth. If the train is on time you may have a few minutes to look around the station. Out the front you'll find a garden of edible plants – planted and looked after by volunteers, locals are invited to pick plants when they are ripe. Yum!

Dovey Junction/Cyffordd Dyfi

If you sit on the left-hand side of the train between Machynlleth and Dovey Junction you may spot an osprey or two. It's a known nesting site for the birds.

Below | Artwork at Newtown/ Drenewydd created by young people from the local school.

Aberystwyth

You don't even have to leave the station at Aberystwyth to make a visit to the Vale of Rheidol Railway. A narrow-gauge steam railway, the journey from Aberystwyth to Devil's Bridge along the Vale of Rheidol is just over 11 miles. Between 1948 and 1989 the line became the only steam railway managed by British Rail as part of the national network. It even survived the 1960s Beeching cuts! The line takes you through some of the most scenic countryside in North Wales and is definitely worth a trip.

Dovey Junction/Cyffordd Dyfi

The next stage of this route will take you back to Dovey Junction, where you change trains to make your way further up the north-west coast of Wales.

Dovey Junction is one of the remotest stations in Wales, located between Dyfi National Nature Reserve and the southern tip of Snowdonia National Park. The scenery is just stunning. Changing here, you

Below | Delicious! Edible plants, grown and looked after by volunteers at Machynlleth to encourage support for local produce and healthy eating.

get a few minutes to absorb the landscape while you wait for the Pwll-heli train to pull in.

Tywyn

If you alight at Tywyn station you are no more than 600 yards away from another great Welsh miniature railway. The Talyllyn Railway claims to be the world's first preserved railway and will take you on a journey through the Fathew Valley in Snowdonia National Park.

Above | We believe every station should have its own guerrilla knitters.

Opposite | The majestic views of Snowdonia from Harlech station footbridge.

Llwyngwril

Look out for some impressive guerrilla knitting on the platform at Llwyngwril station, created by local yarn bombers – as well as Daleks there are also trains and witches, and there are even more to see throughout the village.

Barmouth/Abermaw

If you've been snoozing up until this point you'd better set your alarm, or have the guard wake you up, so you can enjoy one of the most incredible views on the entire British rail network: Barmouth Bridge/Pont Abermaw.

The viaduct is a Grade II listed structure that crosses the River Mawddach. It is made mainly from wood, which means it's a costly piece of infrastructure to maintain, but its importance to the local area outweighs the monetary concerns. As well as by railway, you can also cross the bridge as a cyclist or pedestrian.

The town of Barmouth itself boasts impressive seaside views and beaches, quaint buildings and streets in the old town and historic sites that highlight the town's shipbuilding history.

Llandanwg

If you like a good ramble you may enjoy, as Geoff did, taking a walk between Llandanwg and Harlech. The journey is about two miles along country lanes, so do watch out for traffic, but the views of the coast and Harlech Castle make it well worth the effort.

Harlech

As well as the castle, which we talked about in chapter 1, it is also worth alighting here to absorb the incredible views of Snowdonia from the passenger footbridge.

Also look out for the artwork on the station, another example of young people providing a warm welcome to an area.

Above | Blaenau Ffestiniog –
the heritage railway comes
right into the station. Cross
the bridge to get yourself back
onto the main-line track.

Porthmadog

The town of Porthmadog owes its existence and name to William Madocks, who purchased and reclaimed land around the Glaslyn Estuary, now more commonly known as Porthmadog Harbour. This reshaping of the land led eventually to the development of a railway linking Porthmadog to Blaenau Ffestiniog, where a flourishing slate mine existed. At the time the newly constructed narrow-gauge railway allowed for efficient transportation of slate from the mine to the harbour, where it would be loaded on boats and exported around the world.

The town is home to a bucketload of historically rich buildings and streets, but it is the Ffestiniog Railway that is the real draw here, and a line that we encourage, no, urge you to take.

The scenery along the Ffestiniog Railway is extraordinary. There are several stops along the line, which means you can get on and off and explore the beautiful surrounding countryside (some stops are request only, so make sure to tell the guard before boarding that you'd like to alight).

If you just take a one-way trip, you will end up at Blaenau Ffestiniog station where you can pick up the main-line trains again and continue heading north.

Hope Valley and Buxton Lines

Ardwick – Manchester Piccadilly – New Mills Central – New Mills Newtown – Buxton

Train operating company: Northern

Class of train: 150/156 Sprinter

Wi-Fi: No

Trolley service: No

Friendly guards: Yes!

Views: The Derbyshire hills

Ticket options: A Coast and Peaks Rover lets you have four days of travel in eight, and extends from the peaks to the coasts, including the line down to Buxton and New Mills stations.

In summary: This route will take you from the ultra-urban landscape of Greater Manchester to the idyllic ruminations of rural Derbyshire. The trick here is that you could base yourself at either end of the line, in Manchester or Buxton, and you'd not be disappointed in either.

Ardwick

Ardwick station is not what you would call scenic, but its beauty lies in its limited service and hidden location – don't expect any locals to know where to find the station entrance though. Despite being just one stop up the line from Manchester Piccadilly, only four trains a day (just three when we were travelling in 2017) stop here.

The platforms are overgrown with flowers (some might call them weeds) but there is something appealing about the contrast of nature encroaching on the industrialised infrastructure of the railways. It feels neglected but not in a 'they should bulldoze this down' kind of way, more a 'I could sit here and reflect on life' kind of way.

There is also an incredible view of the city from atop the passenger footbridge, and if you're a train enthusiast there are few quieter places we've found to sit and spot train numbers than at Ardwick.

If you want to squeeze in a visit here your best chance is to start your day on either the 07.34 or the 08.30, which take you directly into Manchester Piccadilly.

Manchester Piccadilly

Manchester Piccadilly station is large and the information displays in the main concourse are VERY confusing. We recommend checking an app or asking a member of staff rather than wasting hours of your life trying to figure out the departure boards. Seriously.

If the departure boards aren't confusing enough, it is also possible to catch a train from here to Manchester Piccadilly (we know!) – it's the service that takes you to Glossop station and then turns around and comes straight back again. It stops at some of the best named stations in the Greater Manchester area including Broadbottom (sniggers), Flowery Field and Godley.

Manchester Piccadilly is one of 19 stations managed directly by Network Rail rather than a local train operating company. As well as catching the train you can also pick up the Manchester Metrolink from the tram stop directly underneath the railway's main platforms. Just

Above | Woodhead New Tunnel plaque, hidden high up on Platform 1.

two stops on the tram will take you into the heart of the city centre and four stops will take you to another of Manchester's impressively large stations, Manchester Victoria.

The station building feels entirely modern, with glassed entrances and modern shopping facilities, but if you look closely there are clues to its heritage. The roof over the platforms is Grade II listed, dating back to 1881, and the columns have wonderful ornate decorations. Tucked high up on the wall of Platform 1 is a little-noticed plaque, commemorating the opening of the Woodhead New Tunnel (the third of three tunnels located on the Woodhead Line between Manchester and Sheffield and now disused) in 1954.

Coming out of Manchester Piccadilly there are three branches of the Hope Valley Line, one via Guide Bridge and Hyde North, another via Belle Vue and the third via Levenshulme. All routes merge in different places, eventually turning into one line around Chinley, after which it ploughs through the Peak District towards Sheffield.

Each of the three routes has different points of interest, but we recommend either the Guide Bridge or Belle Vue options, which lead you through:

Dame
Agatha Christie DBE
1890-1976

MISS MARPLE
Character name inspired by Marple

Unveiled by Mathew Prichard,
grandson of
Agatha Christie

Marple

When we first discovered there was a station called Marple, we were instantly reminded of Agatha Christie's famous crime-solving sleuth, but never really considered that there would be any real connection to the author. How wrong we were.

Evidenced in a letter written to a fan, Agatha Christie visited Marple to purchase some second-hand furniture while in the process of creating a new series of crime novels, and so the name Miss Marple was born. A blue plaque attests to this connection, which was unveiled by Christie's grandson, Mathew Prichard.

The station also celebrates this literary connection through a display of wonderfully vibrant and oversized posters of the Miss Marple novel covers, including *4.50 from Paddington*. A highly suitable railway connection we felt. And a caricature of the lady herself, created by a local artist, can be found on Platform 1.

The Friends of Marple Station are a small but dedicated and active group who run regular events and campaigns to highlight the station and lobby for better services. When we visited, they had approximately 20 members and were looking for newcomers – so if you live in the area . . .

New Mills Central

Between Strines and New Mills Central stations the railway crosses the border between Greater Manchester and Derbyshire. Before 1993 this would not have been the case, but the Cheshire, Derbyshire and Greater Manchester (County and District Boundaries) Order 1993 ruled that the 'area south of Greenclough Farm and north of Woodend, including Whitecroft Farm and part of Station Road' be transferred to Greater Manchester. And this encompassed New Mills Central station.

The station scores a solid eight out of ten on the quaint scale, a rank partially informed by a board just outside the station which highlights the area's connection to another literary figure, Edith Nesbit, who it is said took inspiration from the surrounding countryside for her novel *The Railway Children*. If like us you have watched (and loved) the 1970s film version of the book, you will not be able to help but think of Roberta running down the platform yelling 'My daddy!' when you see the station's stone buildings and surrounding woodland.

The woods are the reason we recommend you alight here to walk the connection to New Mills Newtown station. Look out for the signs for the Torrs Millennium Walkway to get you on your way.

The Millennium Walkway is part of the much longer New Mills Walk. The quickest route between the two stations dissects both of these, but you still get to enjoy some wonderful scenery and views. If you'd like to take an extended ramble, consider carving out some time to pop into the New Mills Heritage and Information Centre in the middle of town to get maps and find out more about the routes.

Above | Torr Vale Mill, a delightful surprise for us as we walked between New Mills Central and New Mills Newtown stations.

To follow our shortened ramble, exit New Mills Central via the ramp at the top of Platform 1, near the passenger footbridge. This will lead you on to Station Road.

Turn right and walk a little way down the road. On your left, you'll see a path taking you into the woodland, with the River Goyt on your right-hand side.

Follow the path, until you reach a fork where the path continues either straight, left or right. Take the right-hand fork, it leads to a bridge which you cross, over the river.

Follow the path (there are some steps on this section), which will lead you around the outside of Torr Vale Mill. An imposing building, thought to be England's longest operational mill having weaved cotton for 215 years, from 1785 to 2000. Originally powered using the might of the River Goyt, it converted to steam power in the 1850s and then to electricity in the 1940s.

With the mill behind you the path will turn into Torrvale and Wirksmoor Road. Follow the road, past all the residential housing, until you reach Albion Road (A6015). Turn right past Swizzels, inventors of Love Hearts, Parma Violets and Rainbow Drops. The Swizzels factory relocated to New Mills in 1940, when the Blitz took its toll on their original factory in east London. Now, New Mills Newtown station is approximately a one-minute walk away.

New Mills Newtown

It feels like a relatively rural station, but New Mills Newtown sees over 204,000 passengers every year. From here catch a southbound train towards Buxton.

Chapel-en-le-Frith

The town of Chapel-en-le-Frith boasts origins dating back to the twelfth century. The name is said to come from the French, meaning 'chapel in the forest'.

At the station look out for heritage-style signage which claims the town to be 'Home of Ferodo' (not Frodo, as we originally thought). Ferodo are a company internationally renowned for their transport braking systems. They started by making brakes for horse-drawn carts in the late nineteenth century, later moving into motorised vehicles.

Buxton

The first thing you'll notice when you arrive at Buxton station is the Grade II listed 'fan window' located at the far end of the platforms (next to the buffers). It is the original London and North Western Railway station wall, built in 1863 and recently restored. On the opposite side of the road there had been a second fan window attached to the building of the town's second station, owned and run by Midland Railway. We know of no other examples on the British Rail network of two

'From the ultra-urban landscape of Greater Manchester to the idyllic ruminations of rural Derbyshire'

stations, adjacent to each other, with identical buildings, run by different companies. Their designs are often credited to Joseph Paxton (the man responsible for Crystal Palace, and bizarrely he cultivated the Cavendish banana too!); however, Historic England clarifies that technically the design was created by John Smith, but *advised* by Paxton.

You need only walk five minutes from the station to find yourself in the centre of town where the feature attraction is The Crescent. Built for the Fifth Duke of Devonshire (why he was living in Derbyshire we don't know) as part of his plan to turn Buxton into a popular Georgian spa retreat. The Crescent was originally made up of a hotel, residential accommodation and a very popular public assembly hall. Today it is under redevelopment having gained several multimillion-pound investments. If you visit any time before 2019 expect to see a lot of scaffolding where elegant Georgian architecture should be.

But don't be put off by the construction – there is so much to do in Buxton. You may want to consider an overnight stay. One location we didn't have time for but would love to go back to was Poole's Cavern – an underground limestone cave that tells a very difficult story of architecture and construction.

By far the best thing about the town, however, or so we think, is St Ann's Well, where you can fill up your own bottles with fresh mineral water from Buxton's natural spring.

Below | The views from the train get particularly impressive on the way down to Buxton.

London Overground

Rotherhithe – Highbury & Islington – Richmond

Train operating company: London Overground
Class of train: 378 Capitalstar
Wi-Fi: At stations only
Trolley service: No
Friendly guards: Staff are friendly, but no guards on trains.
View: Cityscape
Ticket options: Use a TfL Oyster Card or a contactless bank card.

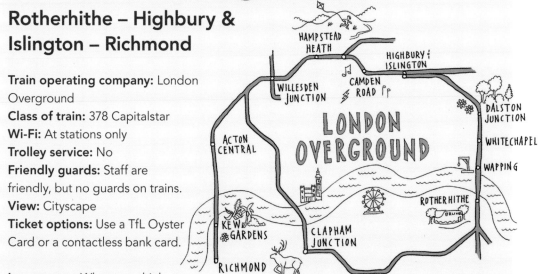

In summary: When you think of travelling in London, almost certainly you'll think about using the Underground. But we would like to recommend the lesser-considered London Overground. Even though services are run by Transport for London (TfL) and the line appears on the Tube map, it is in fact part of the National Rail network and is a great way to explore some of London's Zone 2–4 locations. While parts of it are beneath ground, as the name suggests you get to see much more of London's skyline and city landscapes than you would by Tube. You could choose one place to alight to make the entire journey in just one day. But why not choose two or even three locations, and make a weekend of it?

Rotherhithe

We defy anyone to miss the opportunity to visit the Brunel Museum. As you exit the station at Rotherhithe, turn immediately left and left again and walk along Railway Avenue (no joke!). The first thing that will catch your eye is a round building, surrounded by gardens and sporting an inviting black and white mural of figures digging and working inside a tunnel. Not just any tunnel, the Thames Tunnel is London's and the world's first tunnel to be constructed underneath a river. It is considered by some, including museum director Robert Hulse, to be the eighth wonder of the world, and its construction started here.

Opposite | The Brunel Tunnel shaft, looking more striking now than when it was originally built.

The museum tells the story of the tunnel from conception to completion in 1843, and through it you learn of the ingenuity, bravery and ambition of the Brunel family. For it wasn't just the famous Isambard Kingdom who was involved, but also his father Sir Marc.

The most impressive part of the museum, however, must be the Grand Entrance Hall, the round building you see on your approach to the museum. This is the initial shaft, sunk 50 feet into the ground, which started the tunnel construction and later, when the tunnel was complete, became a hugely popular visitor attraction, as it is now. Through recent funding the shaft is once again open to the public for exploration and events, including musical performances. Apparently, a tunnel shaft offers the perfect acoustic setting for an evening of entertainment. Who knew?!

You can even ride through the Thames Tunnel, not as part of any specific museum event or prearranged tour, but because it still forms part of the Overground network 175 years on. Just jump back on the train and head north, immediately as the train leaves Rotherhithe station press your face against the window to peer into the darkness. If you're looking on the right-hand side you'll see brick arches whizz past: this is the Thames Tunnel.

Wapping

If you alight at Wapping take a few moments on the platform to look up and notice the enduring Victorian brickwork. Then look towards the end of the platform and absorb the incredible craftsmanship of the entrance to the Thames Tunnel. When you feel suitably impressed, head on up the stairs and out of the station.

Wapping is steeped in Docklands history. The station is situated on Wapping High Street, just a stone's throw from the shore of the Thames. Cobbled streets and tall warehouses evoke a feeling of industrial east London.

As a major port it wasn't only goods that made their way up the river – smugglers and pirates were also aplenty in this part of London. Indeed, many a dark story is connected to their activities, none perhaps as gruesome as Execution Dock – located along the Thames (its exact location is still debated) and where the Admiralty carried out their laws of justice. Anyone who had committed a crime at sea, no matter who they were or where it had taken place, could be punished here. If found guilty the perpetrator would be hung over the shoreline.

'Buildings of historic, social and cultural significance'

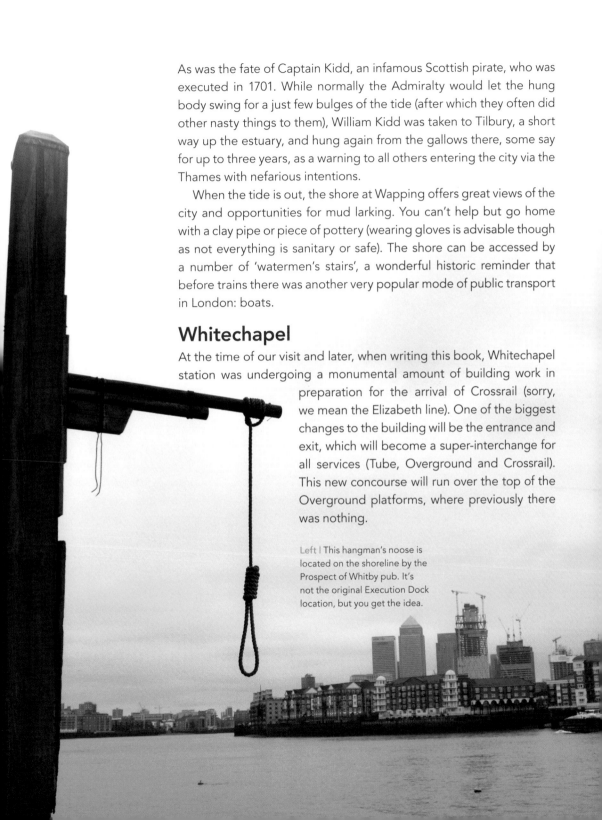

As was the fate of Captain Kidd, an infamous Scottish pirate, who was executed in 1701. While normally the Admiralty would let the hung body swing for a just few bulges of the tide (after which they often did other nasty things to them), William Kidd was taken to Tilbury, a short way up the estuary, and hung again from the gallows there, some say for up to three years, as a warning to all others entering the city via the Thames with nefarious intentions.

When the tide is out, the shore at Wapping offers great views of the city and opportunities for mud larking. You can't help but go home with a clay pipe or piece of pottery (wearing gloves is advisable though as not everything is sanitary or safe). The shore can be accessed by a number of 'watermen's stairs', a wonderful historic reminder that before trains there was another very popular mode of public transport in London: boats.

Whitechapel

At the time of our visit and later, when writing this book, Whitechapel station was undergoing a monumental amount of building work in preparation for the arrival of Crossrail (sorry, we mean the Elizabeth line). One of the biggest changes to the building will be the entrance and exit, which will become a super-interchange for all services (Tube, Overground and Crossrail). This new concourse will run over the top of the Overground platforms, where previously there was nothing.

Left | This hangman's noose is located on the shoreline by the Prospect of Whitby pub. It's not the original Execution Dock location, but you get the idea.

Whether you visit Whitechapel before or after the new station is in operation, you can't fail to fall in love with the vibrancy and bustle of this part of London. Since Roman times Whitechapel has been a key location along one of the major routes in and out of the city. Cultures and languages from all over the world are tangible here as you walk through the streets.

A wonderful place to uncover much of the history of the area is the world-famous Brick Lane. Perhaps best known for its curry houses, Brick Lane is also home to several stops along the Tower Hamlet's 'Cultural Trail'. You can simply follow the street signs and information boards, or you can download more detailed information from the Tower Hamlets website. Either way, we recommend you factor in some time to see Brick Lane's Jamme Masjid, on the corner of Fournier Street. Originally a French Huguenot chapel in 1743, then a Methodist chapel and later a synagogue, the building became a mosque in 1976. The mosque's minaret, which calls people to prayer, is one of the newest icons along the lane. The integration of different faiths in Whitechapel is a symbol of the many influences that make the area an exciting place to explore.

The Truman Brewery is also worth a visit. Brewing on this site dates to the seventeenth century, and the accompanying buildings are some of the finest examples of their kind in London. Today the Truman complex is a mix of offices, shops and galleries.

Deviate into any of the surrounding streets, courtyards and avenues and you'll find buildings of historic, social and cultural significance. Take Princelet Street, for example, where if you're keen enough of eye you'll spot a blue plaque commemorating the birthplace of Miriam Moses, the first female mayor of Stepney.

Continue to the end of Brick Lane and then turn left onto Bethnal Green Road; just a short walk away is Shoreditch High Street station, where you can jump right back on the train.

Below | A great reflection of the local cultures, you'll find nearly every street sign adjacent to Brick Lane is in both English and Bengali.

Dalston Junction

Green spaces in this part of London are few and far between, but a real gem can be found just seconds away from Dalston Junction station. The Dalston Eastern Curve Garden is situated on a former curve of railway track, originally part of the little-known North London Railway in the nineteenth century.

The Curve Garden was established in 2010 and is a welcoming and relaxing community space, particularly if you've been travelling on the rails all day. Events and workshops are run throughout the year and volunteer gardeners help to keep everything growing. You can enjoy the wonderful flourishing plants, a cuppa and slice of cake from the café, and even something stronger in the evenings.

Highbury & Islington

Highbury & Islington is the end of the line for this stretch of the Overground. To keep following our suggested route you'll have to change trains here. Trains from Dalston come in on either Platforms 1 or 2. If you've arrived on Platform 1, you'll need to cross over the footbridge to Platform 7 for the Overground line to where we're going next. If you've arrived on Platform 2, then it's the adjacent platform that you want, and you can just walk across. Take the first westbound train that comes along.

Below I Camden Town, we mean Camden Road station.

Camden Road

The current Camden Road station is a Grade II listed building. It opened in 1870 as Camden Town, and its name changed in 1950. The current Camden Town station (part of the London Underground Northern line) is located five minutes' walk away along the Camden Road. If you look at the exterior of the building though – high up – you'll see an old sign in the brickwork that says 'Camden Town'. No wonder people still get confused and head to the wrong station!

If you have some time to explore, walk towards the Tube station and then make your way up Camden High Street to soak in the full Camden experience: the boutiques, the music, the street food and the traffic. At the top of the High Street, just after you cross the Regent's Canal, are the Camden Lock and Camden Stables markets, probably two of the most famous markets in the city.

Besides all the great bargains and conversations to be had with stall holders, take note of the cobbled floors and arches. It's called the Stables Market because it was once home to over 400 horses, who pulled boats along the Regent's Canal and shifted goods from the railway depot next door. There was even a horse hospital to look after the sick and injured. It is incredible to think that this now vibrant and creative artisan hub was once one of the most industrial areas of the city.

To continue along our route, make your way back to Camden Road and pick up another westbound train.

Hampstead Heath

The most obvious thing to do when you reach Hampstead Heath is visit Hampstead Heath (it's almost directly opposite the station). And don't let us put you off. It's a great heath – the view from atop Parliament Hill is particularly awesome and well worth the steep climb.

However, can we persuade you to veer past the entrance to the heath and continue along South End Road, turning left into Keats

Below | Who can resist the view from Parliament Hill.

Grove? You'll not be disappointed, as 150 yards along you'll find the picturesque Keats House.

John Keats didn't own the house, nor was he born or did he die here, he simply stayed here as a lodger for a mere 17 months. However, these 17 months were arguably some of the most poetically productive of his career and it was also here that he met and fell in love with Fanny Brawne, literally the girl next door.

You can find out more about Keats and how he spent his time in Hampstead through the exhibits and artefacts on display. There are also lots of literary events that take place throughout the year, so it's worth checking the calendar before you make a visit.

When you get back on the train at Hampstead Heath make sure to take a look out the window between the next few stops. Along this part of the line you really start to notice how the Overground ducks and weaves under, over and alongside buildings, secreting itself into the very fabric of the city.

Willesden Junction

If you picked up the Clapham Junction train at your last stop, now change (staying on the same platform) and catch a train heading for Richmond instead.

Kew Gardens

On the approach to Kew Gardens the railway takes you across the Thames. If you look to your right you'll see Oliver's Island (which legend would have you believe was a one-time hide out for Oliver Cromwell), and to the left an unimpeded view of the river.

We like it when a station name tells you exactly where it is they are taking you. Though Kew Gardens is more colloquial: their official title is Royal Botanic Gardens Kew. If you make a visit (it's only a five-minute walk from the station) expect exotic plants but also art installations that focus on specific aspects of the natural world. For example, The Hive designed by Wolfgang Buttress. This aluminium structure, 17 metres (nearly 56 feet) tall, is connected to a real hive within the gardens. Every movement made by the bees is transmitted directly to the installation, and reverberates and amplifies around you. When you're standing in the middle of The Hive there is something wonderfully calming and natural about this very unnatural experience.

Richmond

Richmond station is another of London's multi-service transport hubs. South Western Railway, the Underground and the Overground all stop here. If you make this the last stop on your adventure, you'll have multiple transport options for the journey home.

As a town, Richmond has always had a strong connection to royalty. Henry VII may have built a palace, but it was Charles I who officially introduced deer to the area and created what we know now as Richmond Park.

The quickest way to reach the park from the station is to take the 371 bus from right outside, go ten stops and alight at 'American University'. Just three minutes' walk around the corner and you'll enter the park via Richmond Gate.

Richmond Park is one of eight Royal Parks in London and one of only two National Nature Reserves in Greater London (Ruislip Woods is the second). It is no exaggeration to say that the landscape and wildlife in Richmond are truly awe-inspiring. The second you pass through the gate it's as if urban London no longer exists. The sounds of the city fade and thousands of animals freely wander through its 2,500 acres of land, including us humans.

Deer play a huge role in the life of the park, and are a big draw for the public. During our visit we felt very lucky to see them grazing only a short distance away from us, but they can be dangerous so we'd advocate not approaching them.

Right | Deer casually grazing as visitors wander past transfixed.

Cumbrian Coast Line

Barrow-in-Furness – Carlisle

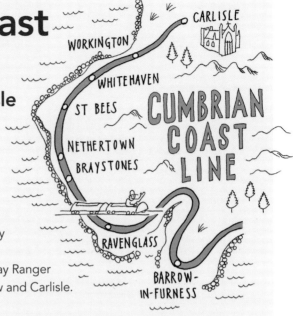

Train operating company: Northern
Class of train: Pacer (yay!) or Class 37
(a 'proper' train)
Wi-Fi: No
Trolley service: No
Friendly guards: Yes!
Views: Yes, jaw-dropping ones, particularly overlooking the coast.
Ticket options: Get the Cumbria Coast Day Ranger for unlimited travel all day between Barrow and Carlisle.

In summary: You can easily do the whole line in one day without stopping, but with a careful bit of timetable checking you could explore more places by going back-and-forth along the line and not just constantly heading in one direction. If you time your journey just right, you might also pick up the loco-hauled Class 37. If you pick up a physical copy of the timetable from the ticket office, all the 'Tractor' services will be marked. Cracking views and likely a sharp breeze coming in from the coast, wrap up warm!

Barrow-in-Furness

The station is located almost on the tip of Cumbria's Furness peninsula and is one of two 'in-Furness' stations along the first part of the line (the second is Kirkby-in-Furness). Originally known as 'Barrow Central', this station used to be the terminus of the line, and was once even serviced by sleeper trains from London; alas no more.

If you buy your ranger ticket here, take a few moments to observe the poignant war memorial that's in the ticket hall. And then as you head for the train, take another moment to admire the array of semaphore signalling that's still evident from the platforms.

The first part of the journey brings you in sight of many wonderful views. Especially look out for the bridge between Foxfield and Green Road stations.

'Admire the array of semaphore signalling that's still evident'

Ravenglass

As the train pulls into Ravenglass station it is immediately obvious what it is you can do here and why you should definitely consider alighting. The Ravenglass & Eskdale miniature steam railway is located right next to the main-line station and is an incredible seven-miles long. It takes 40 minutes to make the journey from Ravenglass to Dalegarth stations, and the views alongside the River Mite are just superb.

The railway has a brilliant colloquial name too, La'al Ratty, which we are told means 'little railway'. The line was originally a three-foot gauge, but was later converted down to fifteen inches. There are seven request stops along the line, lots of excellent opportunities to get out at one of them and take a countryside walk to the next. To be honest, you could easily spend an entire day travelling up or down the line and then afterwards perhaps pop into the Ratty Arms for a celebratory beverage.

As and when you rejoin the journey and continue north, admire the coastal views out of the left-hand side of the train, but don't forget to keep an eye out for Sellafield nuclear reprocessing plant on the right as you travel between Seascale and Sellafield stations. The whole area along this section of the line has a long history of nuclear production, including the now non-operational Calder Hall, which boasted the 'accolade' of being the world's first commercial nuclear power station.

Above | Sellafield. It is as bleak as it looks, we're afraid.

It's quite likely that workers from the plant will be getting on and off the train at Sellafield, but you want to stay on until Braystones.

Braystones and Nethertown

We highly recommend you walk between two of the most isolated stations along the line. Both stations are request stops, so make sure to check the timetable carefully as not all services will stop. If you plan it right though, it can be done.

It's also worth checking ahead for the tidal patterns, as it takes about an hour to walk leisurely along the beach between the stations and you don't want to get cut off. Oh, that's right, the beach! There is a small road that runs parallel with the seafront, but it disappears three quarters of the way there, after which the most direct route is to drop back down onto the beach. (There isn't even Google Street View to check road conditions, you are really in the country now.) Whatever way you do it, take your time to enjoy crashing waves along the shore and wonder, 'Who lives here?' as you see a tiny bungalow, all by itself.

When you reach Nethertown station the platform is tiny, with a Harrington Hump (a ramped section of platform installed to decrease the depth of the step between the train and platform edge, given its name by the station where it was first trialled) that takes up half the length of the platform. To quote Geoff, 'It's a new level of nothingness.'

St Bees

You be forgiven for thinking that, with a name like St Bees, the motto or symbol of the local village will be a bee. While bees are eminently amazing, there is an even more incredible story associated with this place.

It is said that St Bega was the daughter of an Irish king. She refused to marry the man her father had chosen for her and so she ran away, ending up here on the Cumbrian coast where she spent much of her time in religious seclusion. A sculpture of St Bega stands in a small garden right next to the station.

St Bees' beach is a big attraction for visitors, with stunning views of the coast and surrounding landscapes. We spoke to lots of families on the train heading to the beach with their buckets and spades.

Just another five minutes' walk from the station there is St Bees Priory, home of the famous St Bees Man. This story dates back to the fourteenth century, but actually starts in 1981, when a group of archaeologists began digging under the priory car park (what is it with people slapping car parks over prominent English burial sites?). Not long into the dig the group unexpectedly discovered a stone-

Below | The current station building at St Bees dates from 1860, although the very first station opened here in 1849.

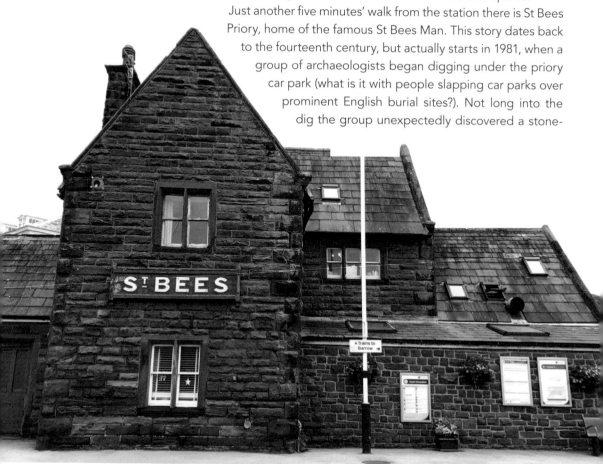

lined vault positioned close to where the priory's original altar would have been. Inside the vault was the skeleton of a woman and a lead-lined coffin containing the almost flawlessly preserved body of a man.

Inside the priory is a comprehensive display of images and objects related to the St Bees Man, with compelling details that unfold about the discovery, the investigation and the eventual conclusion as to who they believe the man to be.

Whitehaven

A trick to visiting Whitehaven is to get out at the station before – Corkickle – which if it didn't already have such a brilliant name could really be called 'Whitehaven South'. You can then walk north through the town towards Whitehaven station. If you have time, do take a small detour to the seafront and the marina. The walk is just over a mile and, if you've ever been curious about naval knots, the marina has sculptures depicting some of the diverse variations that exist – our favourite is the fisherman's loop, which sounds more like a country dance than a knot.

Below | Oh knots! Pardon me, I mean fisherman's loop.

You could even pop into Beacon Museum to discover more about the area's history, which includes two topics we would never have thought of as companions: the Romans and nuclear power. If you're heading in that direction, why not stroll along to the West Pier Lighthouse for some cinematic views? There is a shortcut back to the station – across the front of the marina and over the bridge.

Workington

A traditional market town, with several interesting points of interest to whet the appetite of any history-curious adventurer. We particularly like the sound of pele tower and the Helena Thompson Museum. Interesting railway stories are a very recent occurrence for the people of Workington, when in 2009 the River Derwent burst its banks and washed away all road access between the north side of Workington and the rest of the town. A temporary station – Workington North – was built to help local people get from one side of the town to the other. It took just six days for Network Rail (with help from a few friends in the army and the Royal Engineers) to construct the temporary structure and the shuttle service between Workington and Workington North was provided free of charge! Sadly, there is nothing left to see of the station, but for us it is a great example of the versatility of the railways and how modern engineering techniques can make the unthinkable possible. Could temporary stations be an element of future railway infrastructure to ease overcrowding and congestion?

Besides impromptu railway stations, Workington is also famous for its annual Easter game of 'Uppies and Downies', a medieval version of football played between the two 'sides' of the town. We've watched a YouTube video about it, but we still don't really understand what's going on. Ah, tradition.

Carlisle

When you get to Carlisle station, there's only one thing you have to do, but you really should do it twice. And that's to look up. Crane your head up anywhere within the main part of the station and admire the roof. It was hidden by scaffolding when we visited in 2017 but all the refurbishment work is now complete and we hear it's quite a sight to behold. Once you've done that, go into the tea rooms and look up again, and marvel at the amazing dark-mahogany wooden beams. It feels more like a church than a tea room (or should that be a buffet?). We cannot recall any other café like it on the network.

For a *real* church though, you'll be delighted to know that Carlisle does have a fine cathedral (with its own rather impressive ceiling), and only a few hundred metres away from the station is Carlisle Castle. The castle's history began under William II in the eleventh century and has been the site of many border disputes between England and Scotland over the centuries. Carlisle is also where you can start (or end) your journey along Hadrian's Wall Path.

Opposite | Carlisle station does ceilings well.

Aberdeen to Edinburgh Line

Aberdeen – Stonehaven – Edinburgh

Train operating company: ScotRail
Class of train: 158 / 170 / 220 / 221 / 43 HST
(anything goes!)
Wi-Fi: Yes
Trolley service: Yes
Friendly guards: All ScotRail guards are
friendly!
Views: Incredible coastal views out to the
North Sea, and idyllic farmland of the
lowlands.
Ticket options: No Rover ticket available for
this route, just buy standard single/return tickets.

In summary: The services between Aberdeen
and Dundee and beyond to Edinburgh are
awkwardly scheduled, so it's rare to get a
train that stops everywhere. But if stopping
at all the stations isn't your top priority
(if not, why not?) then this trip becomes easier and you can fit in one or two stops
along the way. Once again this is a line that delivers great views, both on and off the train.

ABERDEEN TO EDINBURGH LINE

Aberdeen/Obar Dheathain

To all intents and purposes, Aberdeen is like any other medium-sized,
busy, city centre station. There are cafés and shops, in fact the station
is linked to the Union Square shopping centre next door, which perhaps gives it a deceptively modern feel. But take a few minutes to look
around and you'll start to notice some eye-catching original features,
such as the iron-framed glass roof.

Oh, we should warn you that the views from the train here as you
leave Aberdeen are beyond describable. So we won't, here's a picture
instead (opposite).

Stonehaven

Frustratingly, during our own journey we didn't have time to venture beyond the station forecourt, but in it we spotted a sign that promised many delights in the town beyond and we urge you take a trip and report back.

The main bay area is about a mile from the station. There are two – that's right TWO – castles, Fetteresso Castle and Dunnottar Castle, both a little way out from the town. Dunnottar Castle is picture perfect, perched on a craggy outcrop teetering over the sea. Evidence from the site dates back to the Picts who lived here before the castle in the third century. That's a lot of history.

There's evidence of activity even further back in time with the Highland Boundary Fault Line, which is just to the north of the town. You can find out even more about the history of the area at the Stonehaven Tolbooth Museum, located in what is thought to be the oldest building in the town. And that's not to mention all the beaches and regular seaside attractions.

Above | Stonehaven town promises a feast of attractions.

Arbroath/Obar Bhrothaig

Geoff: Before our trip I had only ever heard the name Arbroath while listening to the full-time football scores on a Saturday afternoon, waiting for the Pink Panther cartoon to come on TV.

Above | The Declaration of Arbroath as depicted on the platforms of Arbroath station.

'As long as but a hundred of us remain alive, never will we on any conditions be bought under English rule. It is in truth not for glory, nor riches, nor honours, that we are fighting, but for freedom – for that alone, which no honest man gives up but with life itself.'

It's fair to say that Arbroath means a lot more to us now. As soon as you step off the train you get a sense of the historical importance of the area. A large painting on the platforms depicts the 1320 Declaration of Arbroath. The declaration was a milestone towards Scottish independence and its words illustrate the passion and resolve of the Scottish people, led by Robert the Bruce, to reclaim their country from the tyrannical English.

In the background of the portrait you can see a depiction of Arbroath Abbey, which still stands (mostly in ruins) just a few minutes' walk from the station. The abbey was built by William the Lion, William I of Scotland, and it was the presiding abbot at the time who oversaw the drafting of the declaration.

The abbey is also linked to the Stone of Destiny, or Stone of Scone as it's also called. A sacred object, the Stone of Destiny was present at the coronation of Scottish monarchs for many hundreds of years, until the thirteenth century, when Edward I of England stole it and brought it to London. It was subsequently used in English coronations and kept at Westminster Abbey. That is until Christmas Day 1950, when four Scottish students reclaimed the stone and brought it back to Scotland. For three months after it was taken the stone's whereabouts were unknown. It eventually turned up at Arbroath Abbey draped in the Saltire (the Scottish national flag). The stone is now on display at Edinburgh Castle.

Another, what some might consider to be sacred, attraction in Arbroath is Scotland's oldest miniature railway, the delightful Kerr's Miniature Railway. A family run business that's been in operation since 1935, it is situated on the seafront and runs right alongside the main line. You cannot beat that moment when you're on a tiny train and an HST roars past right alongside you.

Barry Links/Machair Bharraidh

There's only one reason why you'd want to come to Barry Links station, and that's because it's now officially the least used in the whole of Great Britain. The latest statistic from the Office of Rail and Road (2016/17) gives Barry Links just 24 recorded journeys for the entire year.

Maths-wise, that's 0.06 people per day, meaning that you're likely to see an actual passenger here about once every two weeks. At the time of writing there are only two opportunities per day to arrive or depart from the station by train, either heading south on the 06.08 to Dundee, or heading north on the 19.12 to Carnoustie.

To spend any time at the station your best bet is to find your way by foot, taxi or bus. But if quiet and quaint stations are your thing, then it's totally worth it. Stand on the platform or the passenger bridge and experience the breeze as a fast train whizzes past.

The word 'Links' and the name of the adjacent station down the line – Golf Street – should be plenty-enough clues to tell you why these stations are here. There are several golf courses nearby including Carnoustie Golf Links, Panmure Golf Club and Monifieth Golf Club. Back in the 1990s there was a significant spike in passenger numbers when the 1999 Open Championship was held at Carnoustie.

Dundee/Dùn Dè

The city of Dundee is packed with history. You could spend weeks here and not see everything. The tip of the iceberg (no pun intended), however, is the RRS *Discovery*, the ship that took explorers Scott and Shackleton to the Antarctic for the very first time. You can explore for yourselves both the ship and the next-door Discovery Point centre to find out more about the stories surrounding this expedition. Both are located directly opposite the station. Also look out for a collection of sad-looking penguins.

Above | Penguins outside Dundee/Dún Dé station, sad or just cold?

Despite the draws of the city, from a railway point of view you'll want to jump back on the train and continue heading south, as this section of the railway crosses the Firth of Tay on the wonderful Tay Rail Bridge.

The current bridge is the second to be built here, the first having come to a tragic end in 1879 when it collapsed during a storm while a passenger train was on top of it. Over 70 people lost their lives. The rebuilt bridge, designed to much higher safety standards, opened in 1887 and was strengthened further in 2003. Today it is one of the many highlights of this part of the network, providing Instagram-worthy views from all directions.

North Queensferry/Port na Banrighinn

For a more cheerful bridge story, there's possibly nothing better than crossing or getting a close look at the Forth Bridge, located across the Firth of Forth between North Queensferry and Dalmeny stations.

Get off the train at North Queensferry and make your way out of the station. Turn right along Ferryhill Road (there used to be a ferry here, not right by the station of course, but this was the road that led you to the ferry crossing). Keep going down the hill and when you reach the end of the road turn left onto Main Street and then another left into Battery Road. Walk as far as you can, up to the point where the sign says you can go no further, and now you're exactly where you need to be, standing directly *beneath* the Forth Bridge and trust us there is no better view of it.

Below | You can catch a teasing glimpse of the Forth Bridge from North Queensferry station. But this is nothing compared to the views across it.

Edinburgh

The final stop on this line is Edinburgh Waverley. You could alight at Edinburgh Haymarket, but that leaves you a little bit further outside of the main action of the city.

We cannot recommend Edinburgh to you enough. As you take time to wander around you'll notice a distinct difference between the north and south side of the city, divided by – you guessed it – the railway. On the south side the architecture feels overwhelmingly gothic. The Royal Mile is a perfect example with its cobbled pavements, exceedingly tall buildings and the Cathedral of St Giles at its heart. Narrow closes and alleys create a network of passageways, some linking higher and lower levels of the streets without at first much obvious logic. You'll feel as if you are forever going uphill. On the north side is Princes Street, the main shopping area that includes all your typical high street chains, cafés and restaurants.

Anything we write will not even start to scratch the surface of what is on offer so instead here is our top five of things to do while in the city:

1 Walk the Royal Mile and visit the castle – of course!
2 Climb Arthur's Seat.
3 Go underground to explore the hidden city under the streets at Real Mary King's Close.
4 Take a ride on the trams.
5 Visit the Scottish Storytelling Centre for some cultural immersion.

Below | The view from the top of Arthur's Seat, an extinct volcano that looks out across the city. There are multiple routes to the top, all are well worth the effort.

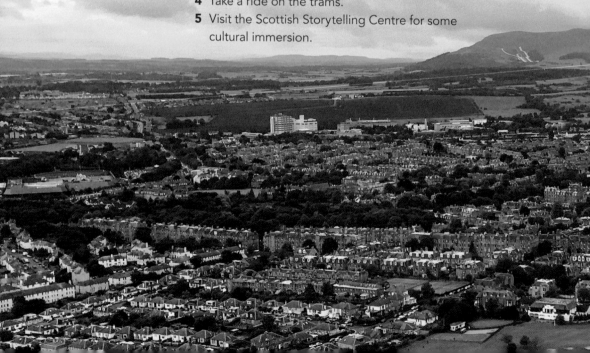

Least-served stations

One train a week: Bordesley (unless for special occasions), Teesside Airport

Two trains a week: Denton, Pilning, Reddish South

Six trains a week: Polesworth, Heysham Port, Gainsborough Central, Kirton Lindsey, Brigg

Seven trains a week: Shippea Hill

Eight trains a week: Buckenham

Nine trains a week: Lakenheath

Ten trains a week: Coombe Junction Halt, Finstock, Ascott-under-Wychwood

Eleven trains a week: Redcar British Steel

Twelve trains a week: Chathill, Clifton, Elton & Orston, Breich, Balmossie, Barry Links, Golf Street

MOST-comfy trains

1 Class 68 – diesel-hauled, run by Chiltern Railways
2 Class 222 – Merdian units, run by East Midland Trains
3 Class 159 – Sprinter, refurbished and run by South Western Railway
4 Class 319 – run by Northern
5 Class 90 – diesel-hauled, run by Greater Anglia

LEAST-comfy trains

1 Class 142, 143 and 144 – Pacers (bouncy!)
2 Class 700 – Thameslink trains (have been compared to ironing boards)
3 Class 220/221 – Voyager, CrossCountry Trains

ALL THE STATS

Did we mention, we're not trainspotters? It's true. Believe it or not, we didn't write down one train number during our journey. We did, however, write down a whole bunch of other facts and figures about our journey and the railways in general. If you're a secret statistics nerd then these two pages are just for you (you're welcome).

Number of trains we travelled on: 622.
Only 17 of them were late/cancelled, which means that 97.3 per cent of our trains ran to time.

Classes of trains we travelled on: we travelled on every class of train in Britain – *except* for the Class 155 Sprinter. Only a few units of these remain now in the Leeds/Bradford area and we didn't get to travel on one.

Train operating companies we travelled on: 24
Arriva Trains Wales, c2c, Caledonian Sleeper, Chiltern Railways, CrossCountry, East Midland Trains, Greater Anglia, GWR, Heathrow Connect, Heathrow Express, London Midland, London Overground, Merseyrail, Northern, ScotRail, Southeastern, Southern, Thameslink, Great Northern, South West Trains, TfL Rail, TransPennine Express, Virgin Trains West Coast, Virgin Trains East Coast.

South West Trains have since become South Western Railway. London Midland have since become West Midland Trains, which is split into two brands: London NorthWestern Railway and West Midlands Railway. Since July 2018 Virgin East Coast franchise has become LNER – London North Eastern Railway. Arriva Trains Wales franchise will change to being run by KeolisAmey Wales in October 2018.

Best station names

1 Poppleton
2 Giggleswick
3 Barry Links
4 Llanfairpwllgwyngyllgogerych-
   wyrndrowllllantysiliogogogoch
5 Hag Fold
6 Hall i' th' Wood
7 Grindleford
8 Sandwich
9 Ulleskelf
10 Corkickle

Train operating companies not travelled on: 3
Gatwick Express, Grand Central, Hull Trains

Train operator we travelled on the most: Northern

Train operator we travelled on the least:
Heathrow Connect/Express

Milestones

We travelled to 2,563 stations

One third of the way through: Station 854 – Lakenheath

Halfway through: Station 1,281 – Shipton

Two thirds of the way through: Station 1,709 – Wallasey Village

Station no. 1,000: Dronfield (between Sheffield and Chesterfield), visited on 8 June 2017

Station no. 2,000: Mexborough *right* (between Sheffield and Doncaster), visited on 20 July 2017

Since completing all 2,563 stations, Kenilworth station opened to become number 2,564, Corfe Castle is being counted by the Office of Rail and Road as station number 2,565 and Maghull North opened on the 18 June 2018 to become station number 2,566.

Station arrived at/departed from the most: Glasgow Central *left* (12 times)

Most stations travelled to in one day: on the 17 May 2017, in Kent, we travelled to 81 stations including Maidstone (West and East), Ashford, Paddock Wood, Sevenoaks, Swanley and Rochester.

The ten counties with the most stations:

Greater London – 333

Kent – 105

Greater Manchester – 92

Surrey – 84

Merseyside – 80

Essex – 74

West Midlands – 69

West Yorkshire – 69

Lancashire – 62

North Yorkshire – 62

Request stops

There are 147 request stops in Great Britain:

Wales – 65 (44%)

England – 60 (41%)

Scotland – 22 (15%)

REFERENCES

Much of our knowledge and understanding has come from the experience of visiting the places we describe, talking to people and asking lots of questions along the way. Our thanks to everyone who so generously gave us their time and shared their knowledge with us.

Bibliography

Bownes, David, Oliver Green and Sam Mullins, *Underground: How the Tube Shaped London*, Allen Lane, 2012

Bradley, Simon, *The Railways: Nation, Network and People*, Profile Books, 2016

Camp, Mark, *Rambles from the Railway*, Devon & Cornwall Rail Partnership, 2013

Cowell, Ben, *Runnymede and Magna Carta*, National Trust (Enterprises), 2015

English Heritage Guide Books, *Whitby Abbey*, English Heritage, 2010

Hedley, Olwen, *Windsor Castle*, Robert Hale, 1994

Lumley, Robin, *Tay Bridge Disaster: The People's Story*, The History Press, 2013

McAndrew, Ian and Chris Robson, *St Bees Man*, St Bees Parochial Church Council, 2016

MacIntosh, Jim, *Creating an Edwardian Railway Masterpiece: The Caledonian Railway's Wemyss Bay Station*, Lightmoor Press, Caledonian Railway Association and Friends of Wemyss Bay Station, 2011

Oman, Charles, *Castles*, GWR, London, 1926

Settle Carlisle Railway Development Company, *The Settle Carlisle Railway: A Guide to your Journey*, Settle Carlisle Railway Development Company, 2017

Taylor, Arnold, *Harlech Castle*, Cadw Welsh Historic Monuments, 2007

Wojtczak, Helena, *Railway Women: Exploitation, Betrayal and Triumph in the Workplace*, The Hasting Press, 2005

Woods, Roy, Richard Buxton and Claire Britton, *Rheilffordd Ffeestiniog: Ffestiniog Railway*, Ffestiniog Railway Company, 2016

Online resources

The railways

Association of Community Rail Partnerships *https://communityrail.org.uk*

Carnforth Station Heritage Centre *http://www.carnforthstation.co.uk*

Corrour Station House *https://www.corrour.co.uk/station-house/*

Dartmoor Railway Supporters Association *https://www.dartmoor-railway-sa.org/index.html*

Days Out Guide *https://www.daysoutguide.co.uk*

Derby Conservation Areas: Railways *https://www.derby.gov.uk/media/derbycitycouncil/contentassets/documents/conservationareas/DerbyCityCouncil-RailwayConservationArea.pdf*

Ffestiniog Railway *http://www.festrail.co.uk*

Friends of Reddish South Station *https://friendsofreddishsouthstation.co.uk*
Friends of Wemyss Bay Station *http://friendsofwemyssbaystation.co.uk*
London Transport Museum *https://www.ltmuseum.co.uk*
Market Rasen Heritage Tour *http://www.marketrasenheritagetour.co.uk*
Maw & Co *http://www.mawscraftcentre.co.uk*
Network Rail *https://www.networkrail.co.uk*
North Yorkshire Moors Railway *https://www.nymr.co.uk*
Office of Rail and Road *http://orr.gov.uk*
Parry People Movers *http://friendlycreatives.co.uk/ppm/*
Persons with reduced mobility technical specification for interoperability *https://www.gov.uk/government/publications/persons-with-reduced-mobility-technical-specification-for-interoperability-implementation-plan*
Pilning Station Group *http://www.pilningstation.uk*
Ravenglass and Eskdale Railway *https://ravenglass-railway.co.uk*
Rail Delivery Group *https://www.raildeliverygroup.com*
STEAM Museum *https://www.steam-museum.org.uk*
Strathspey Railway *https://www.strathspeyrailway.co.uk*
Talylln Railway *https://www.talyllyn.co.uk*
The Signal Box *https://signalbox.org*
The Settle–Carlisle Railway *https://www.settle-carlisle.co.uk/about-us/*
Transport Trust *http://www.transporttrust.com*
Vale of Rheidol Railway *https://www.rheidolrailway.co.uk*
West Coast Railways *https://www.westcoastrailways.co.uk*
Wallace#Sewell *http://www.wallacesewell.com*

Places to visit and things to see

Brick Lane Cultural Trail *https://www.towerhamlets.gov.uk/lgnl/leisure_and_culture/local_attractions/cultural_trail/cultural_trail.aspx*
Brunel Museum *http://www.brunel-museum.org.uk*
Buxton Crescent and Thermal Spa *https://buxtoncrescent.com*
Discover Darwin *http://www.discoverdarwin.co.uk*
Discover Derbyshire and the Peak District http://www.derbyshire-peakdistrict.co.uk/index.htm
Dunnottar Castle *https://www.dunnottarcastle.co.uk*
English Heritage *http://www.english-heritage.org.uk*
Haverfordwest Town Museum *http://www.haverfordwest-town-museum.org.uk*
International Slavery Museum *http://www.liverpoolmuseums.org.uk/ism/*
Keats House *https://www.cityoflondon.gov.uk/things-to-do/keats-house/Pages/default.aspx*
Kew Gardens *https://www.kew.org*
Peak District National Park *http://www.peakdistrict.gov.uk/home*

Port Sunlight *http://portsunlightvillage.com*
RRS *Discovery https://www.rrsdiscovery.com*
RSPB Berney Marshes and Breydon Water *https://www.rspb.org.uk/reserves-and-events/*
    reserves-a-z/berney-marshes-breydon-water/
Shrewsbury Castle *http://www.shrewsburymuseum.org.uk/visit-shrewsbury/shrewsbury-castle/*
Scotland Info Guide *https://www.scotlandinfo.eu*
St Bees *www.stbees.org.uk.*
Stirling Castle *https://www.stirlingcastle.scot*
The Beacon Museum, Whitehaven *https://thebeacon-whitehaven.co.uk*
The Royal Parks *https://www.royalparks.org.uk/parks*
The Tower Colliery *http://www.towerregeneration.co.uk*
Torr Vale Mill *https://www.torrvalemill.co.uk*
Undiscovered Scotland *https://www.undiscoveredscotland.co.uk*
Visit Medway *https://www.visitmedway.org*
Visit Scotland *https://www.visitscotland.com*

History

BBC Wales History *http://www.bbc.co.uk/wales/history/*
BBC History *https://www.bbc.co.uk/history*
BBC Scotland's History *http://www.bbc.co.uk/scotland/history/*
British Listed Buildings *https://www.britishlistedbuildings.co.uk*
Department for the Environment, 'The Cheshire, Derbyshire and Greater Manchester (County
    and District Boundaries) Order 1993' *http://www.legislation.gov.uk/uksi/1993/493/made/data.*
    xht?view=snippet&wrap=true
East London History *https://www.eastlondonhistory.co.uk*
Historic England *https://historicengland.org.uk*
Historic Environment Scotland *https://www.historicenvironment.scot*
History Today *https://www.historytoday.com*
Jewish East End *https://www.jewisheastend.com/london.html*
National Records of Scotland, 'The Declaration of Arbroath' *https://www.nrscotland.gov.uk/*
    research/learning/features/the-declaration-of-arbroath
Open Plaques *https://openplaques.org*

General information

RNIB *https://www.rnib.org.uk*
Swizzels *https://swizzels.com*
Ferodo *http://www.ferodo.co.uk*

THANK YOU

Our railway adventure would not have been made possible without the support and dedication of so many people. We would like to say the following thank yous:

Kickstarter backers

All The Stations was made entirely possible by the generosity of 1,564 people who supported us on Kickstarter. Every single contribution made such a difference.

Supporters

We are grateful to the Rail Delivery Group for their endorsement and support throughout our All The Stations journey. Our thanks to the London Transport Museum Friends for their sponsorship of videos and their coverage of our adventure to their members. Also to Mapway for sponsorship of video content in Manchester.

Isle of Wight conspiracy team

The team at mission control kept us and the whole operation going: Lindsey Berthoud, Martin Clitheroe, Steven Francis, Matthew Frost, Dave Green, Ruth Hargreaves, Ken Hawkins, Dan Haythorn, Will Head and Kai Michael Poppe.

Outside broadcast team

En route, we were supported and helped by so many people. We wouldn't have made it without you – in some cases we literally wouldn't have made it on the train!

Gareth Aubrey, Greg Beecroft, Jonathan Bennett, Andy Carter – Calling All Stations, Darren Chapman, Dan Crouch, Karl Florczak, Roger French, Liz Frost, Anthony Goode-Smith, Michelle Goode-Smith, Amelia Green, Richard Griffin, Adam Gripton, Charlotte Guy, Jason Hammond, Joel Hardy, Gareth Hughes, John Kerr, David Kirwin, Helen Lippell, David Mabon, Dave McCormick, Neil McQueen, Tina Onions, Bob Pipe, Gill Pipe, Liz Power, Frank Roach, Dan Spence, Kirsty Walker, Louis Wall, James Wake, Rob Waughman, Matthew Williams, Neil from Warrington and Mark Wringe.

To the book!

Our thanks to everyone who has supported us through the research, and production of this book: Sue Amaradivakara, Alan Barclay, Charlotte Cole, Annette Green, Dave Green, Ruth Hargreaves, Hannah MacDonald, Sarita Mamseri, Ian Marchant, Dave McCormick, Alex Nelson, Sarah Ward.

All the illustrations

Our thanks to Liam Roberts for bringing the rail network to life through his incredible illustrations.

INDEX

of Trains, Stations and Lines

(Page numbers in *italic* type refer to photographs and captions)